*The Story of the 2/4th Oxfordshire &
Buckinghamshire Light Infantry*

THE STORY OF
The 2/4th Oxfordshire and Buckinghamshire Light Infantry

BY
Captain G. K. ROSE, M.C.

WITH A PREFACE BY
Brig.-Genl. the Hon. R. WHITE, C.B., C.M.G., D.S.O.
(late Commander 184th Infantry Brigade)

AND AN INTRODUCTION BY
Colonel W. H. AMES, T.D.

WITH MAPS AND ILLUSTRATIONS BY THE AUTHOR

The Naval & Military Press Ltd

Published by
The Naval & Military Press Ltd
5 Riverside, Brambleside, Bellbrook
Industrial Estate, Uckfield, East Sussex,
TN22 1QQ England

Tel: +44 (0) 1825 749494
Fax: +44 (0) 1825 765701

www.naval-military-press.com
www.nmarchive.com

*In reprinting in facsimile from the original, any imperfections are inevitably reproduced
and the quality may fall short of modern type and cartographic standards.*

LIST OF PLATES

A Soldier of the Battalion	*Cover*
Colonel W. H. Ames, T.D.	*Facing page* 1
Pay-day for 'A' Company	,, ,, 5
Robecq from the South	,, ,, 19
Brigadier-General the Hon. R. White, C.B.	- - 48
A Front-line Post	- - - 69
Company Sergeant-Major E. Brooks, V.C.	- - 101
Vlamertinghe—The Road to Ypres	- - - 128
Hill 35, from an aeroplane photograph	- - - 137
A Street in Arras	- - - 144
'Tank Dump'	- - - 146
In a German gun-pit near Gavrelle	- - - 150
The Canal du Nord at Ytres	- - - 155
Lieut.-Colonel H. E. de R. Wetherall, D.S.O., M.C.	169
Robecq. Old Mill and Bridge	- - - 184
The Headquarters Runners, July, 1918	- - - 199
Corporal A. Wilcox, V.C.	- - - 215
Officers of the Battalion, December, 1918	- - - 218
184th Infantry Brigade Staff	- - - 219
The Adjutant. Cambrai. The Battalion Cooks	- 220
Lieut.-Colonel E. M. Woulfe-Flanagan, C.M.G., D.S.O. R.S.M. W. Hedley, D.C.M. R.Q.M.S. Hedges	221

ILLUSTRATIONS IN THE TEXT

Winchester Trench	- - - - 11
The March to the Somme	- - - - 21
Somme Trench Map	- - - - 37
Maison Ponthieu	- - - - 45
Harbonnières	- - - - 50
The Ablaincourt Sector	- - - - 57
A Duckboarded Communication Trench	- - - 73
The Advance to St. Quentin	- - - - 83
The Raid near St. Quentin	- - - - 95
Arras: The Grande Place	- - - - 110
Noeux Village	- - - - 113
Poperinghe from the West	- - - - 118
The Attack of August 22, 1917	- - - - 123
The Attack on Hill 35	- - - - 133
The Retreat behind the Somme	- - - - 167
Bird's-eye Map of the Robecq Area	- - - - 180
The Nieppe Forest	- - - - 202
Merville Church	- - - - 205
Battalion H.Q. at Chapelle Boom	- - - - 209

CONTENTS

	PAGE
INTRODUCTION	1

CHAPTER I. LAVENTIE, May to October, 1916 - 8

The 61st Division lands in France.—Instruction.—The Laventie sector.—Trench warfare at its height.—Moberly wounded.—B Company's raid.—Front and back areas.—July 19.—Changes in the Battalion.—A Company's raid.—A projected attack.—Laventie days.—Departure for the Somme.

CHAPTER II. THE SOMME BATTLEFIELD, November, 1916 - 19

Departure from Laventie.—At Robecq.—The march southwards.—Rest at Neuvillette.—Contay Wood.—Albert.—New trenches.—Battle conditions.—Relieving the front line.—Desire Trench.—Regina dug-out.—Mud and darkness.—A heavy barrage.—Fortunes of Headquarters.—A painful relief.—Martinsart Wood.

CHAPTER III. CHRISTMAS ON THE SOMME, December, 1916 - 33

The move from Martinsart to Hedauville.—Back to Martinsart.—Working parties.—Dug-outs at Mouquet Farm.—Field Trench.—Return to the front line.—Getting touch.—Guides.—An historic patrol.—Christmas in the trenches.

CHAPTER IV. AT MAISON PONTHIEU, January—February, 1917 - 42

Visitors to the Battalion.—The New Year.—A wintry march.—Arrival at Maison Ponthieu.—Severe weather.—At war with the cold.—Training for offensive action.—By rail to Marcelçave.—Billets at Raincourt.—Reconnoitring the French line near Daniécourt.

CONTENTS.

CHAPTER V. IN THE ABLAINCOURT SECTOR,
February, 1917 - - - - 53
German retreat foreshadowed.—The Battalion takes over the Ablaincourt Sector.—Issues in the making.—Lieutenant Fry mortally wounded.—The raid by German storm-troops on February 28.—The raid explained.

CHAPTER VI. LIFE IN THE FRONT LINE, Winter,
1916—1917 - - - - 67
Ignorance of civilians and non-combatants.—The front line posts.—Hardships and dangers.—Support platoons.—The Company Officers.—The Battalion relieved by the 182nd Brigade.

CHAPTER VII. THE ADVANCE TO ST. QUENTIN,
March to April, 1917. - - - 77
The enemy's retirement.—Road-mending in No-Man's-Land.—The devastated area.—Open warfare.—The Montolu campaign.—Operations on the Omignon river.—The 61st Division relieved before St. Quentin.—End of trench-warfare.

CHAPTER VIII. THE RAID AT FAYET, April, 1917 89
A German vantage-point.—Shell-ridden Holnon.—A night of confusion.—Preparing for the raid of April 28.—The enemy taken by surprise.—The Battalion's first V.C.—The affair at Cepy Farm.

CHAPTER IX. ARRAS AND AFTERWARDS, May,
June, July, 1917 - - - - 103
Relief by the French at St. Quentin.—A new Commanding Officer.—At the Battle of Arras.—Useful work by A Company.—Harassing fire.—A cave-dwelling.—At Bernaville and Noeux.—In G.H.Q. reserve.—A gas alarm by General Hunter Weston.—The Ypres arena.

CHAPTER X. THE THIRD BATTLE OF YPRES,
August, 1917 - - - - 116
A Battalion landmark.—Poperinghe and Ypres.—At Goldfish Château.—The attack near St. Julien on August 22.—Its results.—A mud-locked battle.—The back-area.—Mustard gas.—Pill-box warfare.

CONTENTS. vii

PAGE

CHAPTER XI. THE ATTACK ON HILL 35, September, 1917 - - - - - 132

Iberian, Hill 35, and Gallipoli.—The Battalion ordered to make the seventh attempt against Hill 35.—The task.—A and D Companies selected.—The assembly position.—Gassed by our own side.—Waiting for zero.—The attack.—Considerations governing its failure.—The Battalion quits the Ypres battlefield.

CHAPTER XII. AUTUMN AT ARRAS AND THE MOVE TO CAMBRAI, October, November, December, 1917 - - 142

The Battalion's return to Arras.—A quiet front.—The Brigadier and his staff.—A novelty in tactics.—B Company's raid.—A sudden move.—The Cambrai front.—Havrincourt Wood.—Christmas at Suzanne.

CHAPTER XIII. THE GREAT GERMAN ATTACK OF MARCH 21, January—March, 1918. - - - - - - 156

The French relieved on the St. Quentin front.—The calm before the storm.—A golden age.—The Warwick raid.—The German attack launched.—Defence of Enghien Redoubt.—Counter-attack by the Royal Berks.—Holnon Wood lost.—The battle for the Beauvoir line.—The enemy breaks through.

CHAPTER XIV. THE BRITISH RETREAT, March, 1918 - - - - - - 165

Rear-guard actions.—The Somme crossings.—Bennett relieved by the 20th Division at Voyennes.—Davenport with mixed troops ordered to counter-attack at Ham.—Davenport killed.—The enemy crosses the Somme.—The stand by the 184th Infantry Brigade at Nesle.—Colonel Wetherall wounded.—Counter-attack against La Motte.—Bennett captured.—The Battalion's sacrifice in the great battle.

CHAPTER XV. THE BATTLE OF THE LYS, April —May, 1918 - - - - 173

Effects of the German offensive.—The Battalion amalgamated with the Bucks.—Entrainment for the Merville area.—A dramatic journey.—The enemy break-through on the

viii   CONTENTS.

Lys.—The Battalion marches into action.—The defence of Robecq.—Operations of April 12, 13, 14.—The fight for Baquerolle Farm.—A troublesome flank.—Billeted in St. Venant.—The lunatic asylum.—La Pierrière.—The Robecq sector.

CHAPTER XVI. THE TURNING OF THE TIDE,
            May, June, July, August, 1918 - 192
Rations and the Battalion Transport.—At La Lacque.—The bombing of Aire.—General Mackenzie obliged by his wound to leave the Division.—Return of Colonel Wetherall.—Tripp's Farm on fire.—A mysterious epidemic.—A period of wandering.—The march from Pont Asquin to St. Hilaire.—Nieppe Forest.—Attack by A and B Companies on August 7.—Headquarters gassed.—A new Colonel.—The Battalion goes a-reaping.

CHAPTER XVII. LAST BATTLES, August to December, 1918 - - - - 208
German retreat from the Lys.—Orderly Room and its staff.—The new devastated area.—Itchin Farm, Merville and Neuf Berquin.—Mines and booby-traps.—Advance to the Lys.—Estaires destroyed.—Laventie revisited.—The attack on Junction Post.—Lance-Corporal Wilcox, V.C.—Scavenging at the XI Corps school.—On the Aubers ridge.—The end in sight.—Move to Cambrai.—In action near Bermerain and Maresches.—A fine success.—Domart and Demobilisation.—Work at Etaples.—Off to Egypt.

COMPOSITION OF THE BATTALION ON GOING OVERSEAS - 221
    ,,   ,,   ,,   AT THE ARMISTICE - 222
INDEX   -   -   -   -   -   -   -   -   223

AUTHOR'S PREFACE

My cordial thanks are due to my old Brigadier for his kindness and trouble in writing the Preface, and also to Colonel Ames for contributing the Introduction.

From many friends in the Regiment I have received information and assistance.

This book is based on a series of articles, which appeared in the *Oxford Times* during the summer of 1919. The project, of which this volume is the outcome, was assisted by that newspaper and by the courtesy of its staff.

G. K. ROSE.

OXFORD, November 1919.

PREFACE

My friend, Major G. K. Rose, has set out to describe the doings of the 2/4th Oxfordshire and Buckinghamshire Light Infantry during the Great War.

If I judge his purpose rightly, he designs to paint without exaggeration and without depreciation a picture which shall recall not only now, but more especially in the days to come, the wonderful years during which we ceased to be individuals pursuing the ordinary avocations of life and became indeed a band of brothers, linked together in a common cause and inspired, however subconsciously, by one common hope and interest. If I am correct in my surmise, then I think that Major Rose has written particularly for his comrades of the 2/4th Oxfords and, in a wider sense, of the 184th Infantry Brigade and the 61st Division. And in doing this he seems to me to be performing a great service.

Unfettered by the necessity of drawing an attractive picture and of appealing to the natural desire of the general reader for dramatic and sensational episode, he can rely on his readers to fill in for themselves the emotional and psychological aspects of the narrative. We, his comrades, have but to turn the pages of his story to live again those marvellous days and to feel the hopes and fears, the pathos and the fun, the excitement and the weariness, and the hundred other emotions which gave to life in the Great War a sense of adventure which we can hardly hope to savour again.

It is perhaps right that those who through poor health, age, bad luck or other causes, were unable to leave home and take an active part in the life of the front line, should generously speak of their more fortunate compatriots as 'heroes.' The term is somewhat freely used in these days. I am, however, happy to think that the British officer and soldier is not apt to consider himself in that light and has, indeed, a distinct aversion from being so described. Rather does he pride himself, in his quiet way, on his light-hearted and stoical indifference to danger and discomfort and his power to see the comical and cheery side of even the most appalling incidents in war. Long may this be so.

Viewed in this light, Major Rose's book will in after years give a true picture of the experiences of an English Territorial Battalion in the 'Great Adventure.' Shorn of fictitious glamour, events are narrated as they presented themselves to the regimental officers, non-commissioned officers, and men who bore the heat and burden of the day.

Having said so much, I may be allowed to think that Major Rose is almost too reticent and modest as regards the splendid record of his Battalion.

After the 'big push' of July, 1916, on the Somme, I had the honour to be promoted to the command of the 184th Infantry Brigade, 61st Division. In September I found the Brigade occupying a portion of the line in front of Laventie, just north of Neuve Chapelle. The 61st Division, recently landed from England and before it had had time to 'feel its feet,' had to be pushed into an attack against the enemy's position in front of the Aubers ridge. In this attack it suffered severe losses. The Division, naturally, was burning to 'get its own back.' Unfortunately it had for some weeks to content itself with routine work in the Flanders trenches.

In this connection I may remark that the 61st Division had an unduly large share of the 'dirty work' of demonstrations, secondary operations, and taking over and holding nasty parts of the line. Those who have been through this mill will sympathise, knowing how credit was apt to go to those who took part in the first 'big push' rather than to the luckless ones who had to relieve attacking divisions and take over the so-called trenches which had been won from the enemy. Those trenches had to be consolidated under a constant and accurate bombardment. However, grumbling was not the order of the day, and during the last year of the war the 61st Division came into its own. It received in frequent mentions and thanks from the Commander-in-Chief and the higher command the just reward for its loyal spade work and splendid fighting qualities.

In November, 1916, the 184th Infantry Brigade and the 2/4th Oxford and Bucks Light Infantry found themselves, as the narrative shows, on classic ground near Mouquet Farm. Here I was first thrown into close contact with the Battalion and learned to know and value it. The work was, if you like, mere routine, mere holding the line. But what a line! Shall we ever forget Regina and Desire trenches, with their phenomenal mud and filth; or Rifle Dump and Sixteen Street and Zollern

Redoubt—and Martinsart Wood and the 'rest' there? Names, names! but with what memories!

I am tempted to follow the fortunes of the Battalion through the varied scenes of its experience. I should like to talk of happy mornings 'round the line' with Colonel or Adjutant, or cheery lunches with good comrades in impossibly damp and filthy dug-outs, of midnight assemblies before, and early-morning greetings after, successful raids, and of how we inspected Boche prisoners, machine-guns and other 'loot.'

I should like to recall memories of such comrades as Bellamy and Wetherall, Cuthbert, Bennett, Davenport, 'Slugs' Brown, Rose, 'Bob' Abraham, Regimental Sergeant-Major Douglas, Company Sergeant-Major Brooks, V.C., and a host of other friends of all ranks.

I look back with pride on many stirring incidents.

Among these I recall the raid near St. Quentin on April 28, 1917, admirably planned and carried out by Captain Rose and his company, and resulting in the capture of two machine-guns and prisoners of the 3rd Prussian Jaeger regiment, three companies of which were completely surprised and outflanked by the dashing Oxford assault. On this occasion Company Sergeant-Major Brooks deservedly won the V.C. and added lustre to the grand records of his regiment.

Equally gallant was the fine stand made by the Oxfords on August 22 and 23, 1917, in front of Ypres. Captain Moberly and his brave comrades, surrounded by the enemy and completely isolated,

PREFACE.

stuck doggedly for 48 hours to the trench which marked the furthest point of the Brigade's objective.

Few battalions of the British Army could boast a finer feat of arms than the holding of the Enghien Redoubt by Captain Rowbotham, 2nd Lieutenant Cunningham, Regimental Sergeant-Major Douglas and some 150 men of D Company and Battalion Headquarters. From 10.30 a.m. till 4.30 p.m. on March 21, 1918, these brave soldiers, enormously outnumbered and completely surrounded, stemmed the great tide of the German attack and by their devoted self-sacrifice enabled their comrades to withdraw in good order. 2nd Lieutenant Cunningham, the sole surviving officer for many hours, remained in touch with Brigade Headquarters by buried cable until the last moment. Further resistance being hopeless, he received my instructions, after a truly magnificent defence, to destroy the telephone instruments and cut his way out

But I must not encroach on the domain of our author, a real front line officer, who lived with his men throughout the war under real front line conditions.

It fell to my lot for 18 months to have the Battalion amongst those under my command. Attacking, resting, raiding, marching, the 2/4th Oxfordshire and Buckinghamshire Light Infantry not only upheld but enhanced the glory of the old 43rd and 52nd Regiments of the Line.

ROBERT WHITE,
Brigadier General.

COLONEL W. H. AMES, T.D.

INTRODUCTION

THE raising of the Second Line of the Territorial Force became necessary when it was decided to send the First Line overseas. The Territorial Force was originally intended for home defence, a duty for which its pre-war formations soon ceased to be available. The early purpose, therefore, of the Second Line was to defend this country.

On September 8, 1914, I was privileged to begin to raise the 2/4th Oxfordshire and Buckinghamshire Light Infantry, the Battalion whose history is set out in the following pages. I opened Orderly Room in Exeter College, Oxford, and enrolled recruits. The first was Sergeant-Major T. V. Wood. By the end of the day we had sworn in and billeted over 130 men.

The Battalion was created out of untrained elements, but what the recruits lacked in experience they made up in keenness. The Secretary of the County Association had an excellent list of prospective officers, but these had to learn their work from the beginning. We were lucky to secure the services of several non-commissioned officers with Regular experience; Colour-Sergeants Moore, Williams, Bassett and Waldon, and Sergeant Howland worked untiringly, whilst the keenness of the officers to qualify themselves to instruct their men was beyond praise.

At the end of ten days sufficient recruits had been enrolled to allow the formation of eight companies, which exactly reproduced those of the First Line, men being allotted to the companies according to the locality whence they came. A pleasant feature was the number of Culham students, who came from all parts of England to re-enlist in their old Corps. Well do I remember my feelings when I sat down to post the officers to the companies. It was a sort of 'Blind Hookey,' but seemed to pan out all right in the end. Company officers had to use the same process in the selection of their non-commissioned officers. Of these original appointments all, or nearly all, were amply justified—a fact which said much for the good judgment displayed.

With the approach of the Oxford Michaelmas Term the Battalion had to move out of the colleges (New College, Magdalen, Keble, Exeter, Brasenose and Oriel had hitherto kindly provided accomodation) and into billets. Training was naturally hurried. As soon as the companies could move correctly a series of battalion drills was carried out upon Port Meadow. This drill did a great deal to weld the Battalion together. The elements of digging were imparted by Colonel Waller behind the Headquarters at St. Cross Road, open order was practised on Denman's Farm, whilst exercises in the neighbourhood of Elsfield gave the officers some instruction in outpost duties and in the principles of attack and defence.

The important rudiments of march discipline were soon acquired. Weekly route marches took place almost from the first. Few roads within a radius of 9 miles from Oxford but saw the Battalion some time or other. The Light Infantry step caused discomfort at first, but the Battalion soon learned to take a pride in it. The men did some remarkable marches. Once they marched from the third milestone at the top of Cumnor Hill to the seventh milestone by Tubney Church in 57 minutes. Just before Christmas, 1914, they marched through Nuneham to Culham Station and on to Abingdon, and then back to Oxford through Bagley Wood, without a casualty.

At the end of 1914 Second Line Divisions and Brigades were being formed, and the 2/4th Oxford and Bucks Light Infantry became a unit of the 184th Infantry Brigade under Colonel Ludlow, and of the 61st Division under Lord Salisbury. Those officers inspected the Battalion at Oxford before it left, at the end of January, 1915, for Northampton.

The move from Oxford terminated the first phase in the Battalion's history. At Northampton fresh conditions were in store. Smaller billets and army rations replaced the former system of billets 'with subsistence.' Elementary training was reverted to. The Battalion was armed with Japanese rifles, a handy weapon, if somewhat weak in the stock, and range work commenced. The seven weeks at Northampton, if not exactly relished at the time, greatly helped to pull the Battalion together. The period was marked by a visit of General Sir Ian Hamilton, who inspected and warmly complimented the men on their turn-out.

A minor incident is worthy of record. One Saturday night a surprise alarm took place about midnight. The Battalion was young, and the alarm was taken very seriously. Even the sick turned out rather than be left behind, and marched the prescribed five miles without ill effects.

Just before Easter, 1915, the 61st Division moved into Essex in order to occupy the area vacated by the 48th. The Battalion's destination was Writtle, where the amicable relations already established with the inhabitants by Oxfordshire Territorials were continued. Though our stay was a short one, we received a hearty welcome, when, on our return from Epping, we again marched through the village.

After a fortnight at Writtle, the Battalion moved to Hoddesdon, to take part in digging the London defences. We left Writtle 653 strong at 8 a.m., and completed the march of 25 miles at 5 p.m., with every man in the ranks who started. Three weeks later we were ordered to Broomfield, a village east of Writtle and near Chelmsford. There was keen competition to take part in the return march from Hoddesdon; 685 men started on the 29 mile march, which lasted 11 hours; only 3 fell out. The band marched the whole way and played the Battalion in on its arrvial at Broomfield.

In the spring of 1915 it was decided to prepare the Territorial Second Line for foreign service. Considerable improvement resulted in the issue of training equipment. Boreham range occupied much of our time. A musketry course was begun but never finished; indeed, the bad condition of the rifles made shooting futile. Six weeks were also spent at Epping in useful training, at the conclu-

PAY-DAY FOR "A" COMPANY.

sion of which we returned to Broomfield. The Battalion was billeted over an area about six miles long by one wide, until leave was obtained for a camp. For nearly three months the men were together under canvas, with the very best results. Strenuous training ensued. I am reminded of a little incident which occurred during some night digging at Chignal Smealy. The object of the practice was to enure the men to work, not only when fresh, but when tired. Operations opened with digging with the entrenching tool—each man to make cover for himself. By 8 p.m. this stage had been reached, so tea and shovels were issued. At 9 p.m. serious digging began, the shelters being converted into trenches, and this continued till 1.30 a.m. Coffee was then served, and work went on till dawn, which provided an opportunity to practise standing-to. A rest followed, but after breakfast work was again resumed. About 10 a.m. an officer found a man sitting down in the trenches and ordered him to renew his efforts. The man obeyed the order at once, but was heard to remark to his neighbour, ' Well! If six months ago a bloke had told me that I was a-going to work the 'ole ruddy night and the 'ole ruddy day for one ruddy bob, I'd never 'ave believed him!'

At the end of October, 1915, I consider that the Battalion reached the zenith of its efficiency during its home service. It was a great pity that the Division could not have been sent abroad then. Instead, each battalion was reduced in November to a strength of 17 officers and 600 men. Individual training recommenced, until specialists of every kind flourished and multiplied. At a General's inspection during the winter a most varied display took place. Scouts were in every tree, a filter party was drawing water from the village pond, cold shoeing was being practised at the Transport, cooking classes were busy making field ovens, wire entanglements sprang up on every side, nor was it possible to turn a corner without encountering some fresh form of activity. I fancy the authorities were much impressed on this occasion, for nothing was more difficult than to show the men, as they normally would be, to an inspecting officer.

In January, 1916, the Battalion, having been recently made up with untrained recruits, moved to Parkhouse Camp on Salisbury Plain to complete its training with the rest of the Division. We arrived in frost and snow and left, three months later, in almost tropical heat—remarkable contrasts within so short a period. The Division was speedily completed for foreign service; new rifles were issued, with which a musketry course was successfully fired, though snow showers did not favour high scoring. We were made up to strength with drafts from the Liverpool, Welsh, Dorset, Cambridge, and Hertfordshire Regiments, were inspected by the King, and embarked as a unit of the first Second Line Division to go abroad.

Thus at the end of 18 months' hard work the preparatory stage in the Battalion's history was concluded. Its subsequent life is traced in the chapters of this volume.

The period of home service is wrapped in pleasant memory. It was not always plain sailing, but difficulties were lightened by the wonderful spirit that animated all ranks and the pride which all felt in the Battalion. I recall especially the work of some who have not returned; Davenport, Scott, Stockton, Zeder, and Tiddy among the officers, and among the non-commissioned officers and men a host of good comrades. Nor do I forget those who came safely through. No commanding officer was ever better supported, and my gratitude to them all is unending. I think the Battalion was truly animated by the spirit of the famous standing order, 'A Light Infantry Regiment being expected to approach nearer to perfection than any other, more zeal and attention is required from all ranks in it.' Equally truly was it said that not by the partial exertions of a few, but by the united and steady efforts of all, was the Battalion formed and its discipline created and preserved.

W. H. AMES, *Colonel.*

CHAPTER I.

LAVENTIE.

MAY TO OCTOBER, 1916.

The 61st Division lands in France.—Instruction.—The Laventie sector.—Trench warfare at its height.—Moberly wounded.—B Company's raid.—Front and back areas.—July 19th.—Changes in the Battalion.—A Company's raid.—A projected attack.—Laventie days.—Departure for the Somme.

ON May 24, 1916, the 2/4th Oxfordshire and Buckinghamshire Light Infantry landed in France. Members of the Battalion within a day or two were addressing their first field postcards to England. Active service, of which the prospect had swung, now close, now far, for 18 months, had begun.

The 61st Division, to which the Battalion belonged, concentrated in the Merville area. The usual period of 'instruction' followed. The 2/4th Oxfords went to the Fauquissart sector, east of Laventie. Soon the 61st relieved the Welsh Division, to which it had been temporarily apprenticed, and settled down to hold the line.

It was not long before the Battalion received what is usually termed its 'baptism of fire.' Things were waking up along the front in anticipation of the Franco-British attack on the Somme. Raids took place frequently. Fighting patrols scoured No-Man's-Land each night. In many places at once the enemy's wire was bombarded to shreds. By the end of June an intense feeling of expectancy had developed; activity on both sides reached the highest pitch. The Battalion was not slow in playing its part. One of the early casualties was Lieutenant Moberly, who performed a daring daylight reconnaissance up to the German wire. He was wounded and with great difficulty and only through remarkable pluck regained our lines.

That same night the Battalion did its first raid, by B Company under Hugh Davenport. The raid was ordered at short notice and was a partial success. If the tangible results were few, B Company was very properly thanked for its bravery on this enterprise, which had to be carried out against uncut wire and unsubdued machine-guns. Zeder, a lieutenant with a South African D.C.M., was mortally wounded on the German wire and taken prisoner. The casualties were numerous. Davenport himself was wounded, but unselfishly refused treatment until his men had been fetched in. It was a night of battle and excitement. To the most hardened troops a barrage directed against crowded breastworks was never pleasant. The Battalion bore itself well and earned recital, albeit with some misdescription, in the English press a few days later.

During July 1916 the Battalion was in and out of the breastworks between Fauquissart and Neuve Chapelle. When the 184th Infantry Brigade went back to rest the Battalion had billets on the outskirts of Merville, a friendly little town, since levelled in ruins; and, when reserve to the Brigade, in Laventie. Brigade Headquarters were at the latter and also the quartermasters' stores and transport of battalions in the line.

Some favourite spots were the defensive 'posts,' placed a mile behind the front line and known as Tilleloy, Winchester, Dead End, Picantin. Reserve companies garrisoned these posts. No arduous duties spoilt the days; night work consisted chiefly in pushing trolley-loads of rations to the front line. Of these posts the best remembered would be Winchester, where existed a board bearing the names of Wykhamists, whom chance had led that way. Battalion Headquarters were there for a long time and were comfortable enough with many 'elephant' dug-outs and half a farm-house for a mess—the latter ludicrously decorated by some predecessors with cuttings from *La Vie Parisienne* and other picture papers.

Though conditions were never quiet in the front line, during the summer of 1916 back area shelling was infrequent. Shells fell near Laventie crossroads on most days and, when a 12 inch howitzer established itself behind the village, the Germans retaliated upon it with 5.9s, but otherwise shops and estaminets flourished with national nonchalance. The railway, which ran from La Gorgue to Armentières, was used by night as far as Bac St. Maur—

LAVENTIE, MAY TO OCTOBER, 1916. 11

WINCHESTER TRENCH.

an instance of unenterprise on the part of German gunners. Despite official repudiation, on our side the principle of 'live and let live' was still applied to back areas. Trench warfare, which in the words of a 1915 pamphlet 'could and must cease' had managed to survive that pamphlet and the abortive strategy of the battle of Loos. Until trench warfare ended divisional headquarters were not shelled.

Meanwhile the comparative deadlock in the Somme fighting rendered necessary vigorous measures against the enemy elsewhere on the front. A gas attack from the Fauquissart sector was planned but never carried out. Trench mortars and rifle grenades were continuously employed to make life as unpleasant as possible for the enemy, whose trenches soon became, to all appearances, a rubbish heap. All day and much of the night the 'mediums' fell in and about the German trenches and, it must be confessed, occasionally in our own as well. Whilst endeavouring to annihilate the Wick salient or some such target, one of our heaviest of heavy trench mortars dropped short (perhaps that is too much of a compliment to the particular shot) in our trenches near a company headquarters and almost upon a new concrete refuge, which the R.E. had just completed and not yet shown to the Brigadier. Though sometimes supplied, the co-operation of this arm was never asked for.

This harassing warfare had a crisis in July. The operations of July 19, which were shared with the 61st Division by the 5th Australian holding trenches further north, were designed as a demonstration to assist our attack upon the Somme and to hold opposite to the XI Corps certain German reserves, which, it was feared, would entrain at Lille and be sent south. That object was achieved, but at the cost of severe casualties to the divisions engaged, which were launched in daylight after artillery preparation, which results proved to have been inadequate, against a trench-system strongly manned and garrisoned by very numerous machine-guns. The objectives assigned to the 61st Division were not captured, while the Australians further north, after entering the German trenches and taking prisoners, though they held on tenaciously under heavy counter-attacks, were eventually forced to withdraw. 'The staff work,' said the farewell message from the XI Corps to the 61st Division three months later, 'for these operations was excellent.' Men and officers alike did their utmost to make the attack of July 19 a success, and it behoves all to remember the sacrifice of those who fell with appropriate gratitude. It was probably the last occasion on which large parties of storming infantry were sent forward through 'sally ports.' The Battalion was in reserve for the attack. C Company, which formed a carrying party during the fighting, lost rather heavily, but the rest of the Battalion, though moved hither and thither under heavy shelling, suffered few casualties. When the battle was over, companies relieved part of the line and held the trenches until normal conditions returned.

Soon after these events the Battalion was unlucky to be deprived of Colonel Ames, a leader whose energy and common sense could ill be spared. This was the first change which the Battalion had in its Commanding Officer, and it was much regretted. A change in Adjutant had occurred likewise, Major D. M. Rose having been invalided to England early in July and his place taken by R. F. Cuthbert, formerly commander of D Company. Orderly Room work passed from safe hands into hands equally safe. Soon afterwards I joined the Battalion, having been transferred from the 1/4th, and received command of D Company. The new Commanding Officer, Major R. Bellamy, D.S.O., came from the Royal Sussex Regiment and assumed command early in August. Robinson, an officer from the Middlesex and one of the best the Battalion ever had, Callender and Barton also joined about this time. Brucker, of C Company, became Adjutant of the 61st Divisional School, and command of his company passed to Kenneth Brown, a great fighter and best of comrades, the first member of this Battalion to win the Military Cross. Major Beaman was still Second in Command. Two original officers of the 2/4th, Jack Bennett and Hugh Davenport, commanded A and B Companies respectively. W. A. Hobbs, well known as Mayor of Henley, was Quartermaster, and 'Bob' Abraham the Transport Officer. Regimental Sergeant-Major Douglas and Regimental Quartermaster-Sergeant Hedges were the senior warrant officers.

Higher up a new Brigadier in the person of General Dugan arrived and held command for a short while. The General, I regret to say, did not stay long enough for the full benefit of his experience and geniality to accrue, a fragment of a Stokes' mortar shell wounding him at a demonstration near Merville and causing his retirement to hospital. The new Brigadier, the Hon. R. White, C.M.G., joined us at the beginning of September, 1916, from action on the Somme, and soon made his cheery criticisms felt.

After the operations of July 19 the former methods of trench warfare were resumed. The Division's casualties in the attack had been over 2,000, and time was required to reorganise and make up these losses.

Early in August an unlucky shell deprived the Battalion of one of its best officers. Lieutenant Tiddy had joined the Infantry in a spirit of duty and self-sacrifice, which his service as an officer had proved but to which his death more amply testified. The regrets of friends and comrades measured the Battalion's loss.

At 10 p.m. on August 19 a raid upon the German trenches near the 'Sugar Loaf' was carried out by A Company. The raid was part of an elaborate scheme in which the Australians upon the left and the 2/5th Gloucesters on our own front co-operated. The leading bombing party, which Bennett sent forward under Sergeant Hinton, quickly succeeded in reaching the German parapet and was doing well, when a Mills bomb, dropped or inaccurately thrown, fell amongst the men. The plan was spoilt. A miniature panic ensued, which Bennett and his Sergeant-Major found it difficult to check. As in many raids, a message to retire was passed. The wounded were safely brought in by Bennett, whose control and leadership were worthy of a luckier enterprise.[1]

The Battalion was not called upon for much fighting activity in September, 1916. Raids and rumours of raids kept many of us busy. An attack by the 184th Brigade upon the Wick salient was planned, but somewhat too openly discussed and practised to deceive, I fancy, even the participating infantry into the belief that it was really to take place. Upon the demolished German trenches many raids were made. In the course of these raids, the honour of which was generously shared between all battalions in the Brigade, sometimes by means of the Bangalore Torpedo, sometimes by the easier and more subtle method of just walking into them, the enemy's front line was usually entered; and rarely did a raiding party return without the capture of at least an old bomb, an entrenching tool or even a live German. These 'identification' raids possibly did as much to identify ourselves to the enemy as to identify him to us, but they proved useful occasions on which to send parties 'over the top' (always an enjoyable treat!) and gave practice to our trench mortars, which fired remarkably well and drew down little retaliation—always the bugbear of the trench mortar.

The mention of these things may make dull

[1] A failure of this kind was far less due to any indetermination of the men than to the complex nature of the scheme, which any misadventure was capable of upsetting. On this occasion the 'order to retire' was said to have been of German manufacture, but such explanation deserved a grain of salt. Owing to the danger of its unauthorised use, the word 'retire' was prohibited by Army orders.

reading to the *blasé* warrior of later battlefields, but, as there are some whose last experience abroad was during Laventie days and who may read these lines, I feel bound to recall our old friend (or enemy) the trench mortar, the rent-free (but not rat-free) dugout among the sandbags, the smelly cookhouses, whose improvident fires were the scandal of many a red-hatted visitor to the trenches, the mines, with their population of Colonial miners doing mysterious work in their basements of clay and flinging up a welter of slimy blue sandbags—all these deserve mention, if no more, lest they be too soon forgotten.

Days, too, in Riez Bailleul, Estaires and Merville will be remembered, days rendered vaguely precious by the subsequent destruction of those villages and by lost comrades. Those of the Battalion who fell in 1916 were mostly buried in Laventie and outside Merville. Though both were being fought over in 1918 and many shells fell among the graves, the crosses were not much damaged; inscriptions, if nearly obliterated, were then renewed when, by the opportunity of chance, the Battalion found itself once more crossing the familiar area, before it helped to establish a line upon the redoubtable Aubers ridge, to gain which so many lives at the old 1915 battles of Neuve Chapelle and Festubert had been expended.

It was a fine autumn. The French civilians were getting in their crops within a mile or two of the trenches, while we did a series of tours in the Moated Grange sector, with rest billets at the little village of Riez Bailleul.

And then box respirators were issued.

Laventie days are remembered with affection by old members of the Battalion. In October, 1916, however, there were some not sorry to quit an area, which in winter became one of the wettest and most dismal in France. The Somme battle, which for three months had rumbled in the distance like a huge thunderstorm, was a magnet to attract all divisions in turn. The predictions of the French billet-keepers were realised at the end of October, when the 2/4th Oxfords were relieved in the trenches by a battalion of the Middlesex Regiment and prepared to march southwards to the Somme.

ROBECQ FROM THE SOUTH.

Chapter II.

THE SOMME BATTLEFIELD,

November, 1916.

Departure from Laventie.—At Robecq.—The march southwards.—Rest at Neuvillette.—Contay Wood.—Albert. —New trenches.—Battle conditions.—Relieving the front line.—Desire Trench.—Regina dug-out.—Mud and darkness. —A heavy barrage.—Fortunes of Headquarters.—A painful relief.—Martinsart Wood.

AT the end of October, 1916, the 61st Division left the XI Corps and commenced its march southwards to join the British forces on the Somme. We were among the last battalions to quit the old sector. Our relief was completed during quite a sharp outburst of shelling and trench-mortaring by the enemy, whose observers had doubtless spotted the troops moving up to take over.

After one night in the old billets at Riez Bailleul the Battalion marched on October 29 to Robecq, where the rest of the Brigade had already assembled, and took up its quarters in farms and houses along the Robecq—Calonne road. Battalion Headquarters were established at a large farmstead subsequently known as Gloucester Farm, while to reach the billets allotted to them the companies marched through the farmyard and across the two small bridges, since so familiar to some, which spanned the streams Noc and Clarence. My company was furthest south and almost in Robecq itself; my headquarters were in a comfortable house with an artesian well bubbling up in its front garden. When fighting was taking place at Robecq in April, 1918, and I found myself, under very different circumstances, in command of the Battalion, knowledge of the ground obtained eighteen months before, even to the position of garden gates and the width of ditches, proved most useful. I am afraid the Battalion's old billets were soon knocked down, the favourite estaminet in D Company area being among the first houses to go.

On November 2, 1916, the Battalion left Robecq, where it had been well-housed and happy for a week, for Auchel, a populous village in the mining district, and marched the next day to Magnicourt en Comté, an especially dirty village, and thence again through Tinques and Etrée-Wamin to Neuvillette. The civilians in some of the villages passed were not friendly, the billets crowded and often not yet allotted when the Battalion arrived, having covered its 14 kilometres with full pack and perhaps through rain. Nobody grumbled, for the conditions experienced were normal, but this march with its daily moves involved toil and much footsoreness on the part of the men, and for the officers much hard work after the men were in, and many wakings-up in the night to receive belated orders for the morrow.

After reaching Neuvillette, a pretty village four miles north by west of Doullens, a ten days' rest was made. Boots had become very worn in consequence of the march, and great efforts were now made by Hobbs to procure mending leather;

unfortunately the motor car seemed to have forgotten its poor relation, the boot, and no leather was forthcoming. During the stay at Neuvillette a demonstration in improvised pack saddlery was arranged at Battalion Headquarters, the latest and most disputed methods of wiring and trench-digging were rehearsed, and two really valuable Brigade field days took place. More than a year afterwards the Battalion was again billeted at Neuvillette, whose inhabitants remembered and warmly welcomed the Red Circle.

On November 16 we marched away to Bonneville and the next day reached Contay, where we climbed up to some unfloored huts in a wood. The weather on this march had been bitterly cold, but fine and sunny. A dusky screen of clouds drifted up from the west the evening of our arrival and the same night snow fell heavily. The cookers were not near the huts and neither stores nor proper fuel existed. There was the usual scramble for the few braziers our generous predecessors had left behind. With snow and wind the Battalion tasted its first hardship

As in all such situations, things soon took a cheerful turn. When the General came up next morning, the camp was reeking with smoke from braziers and the smell of cookers and the wood alive with sounds of woodchopping and cries of foragers. This change from a bad look-out to a vigorous optimism and will to make the best of things was characteristic of the British 'Tommy,' who, exhausted and 'fed-up' at night, was heard singing and wood-chopping the next morning, as if wherever he was were the best place in the world. I shall always remember Contay Woods, the huts with their floors of hard mud reinforced by harder tree-stumps, and the slimy path down to parade when we left.

On November 19 we reached Albert, whose familiar church needs no description. What struck me principally on arrival was the battered sordidness of the place and the filthy state of the roads, on which the mud was well up to the ankles. Some civilians were living in the town and doing a brisk trade in souvenir postcards of the overhanging Virgin. Traffic, as always through a main artery supplying the prevalent battlefield, was positively continuous. The first rain of autumn had already fallen and men, horses and vehicles all bore mud-stains significant of winter's approach. Our arrival—we went into empty, rather shell-damaged houses near the station—coincided with the later stages of the Beaumont Hamel offensive, and German prisoners and, of course, British casualties were passing through the town.

At Albert, Bennett was taken from A Company to act as Second in Command of the Berks. Brown assumed command of his company and Robinson about this time of C Company, Brucker having returned to the 61st Divisional School, which was set up at St. Riquier. Just now much sickness occurred among the officers, John Stockton, Moorat and several others being obliged to go away by attacks of trench fever. From Albert C and D Companies moved forward to some Nissen huts near Ovillers to be employed on working parties. For the same duties A and B Companies soon afterwards were sent to Mouquet Farm, while Battalion Headquarters went to Fabick Trench.

24 THE SOMME BATTLEFIELD, NOVEMBER, 1916.

After some rain had fallen, fine autumn weather returned and our guns and aeroplanes were shewing the activity typical of the late stages of a great battle, when future movements were uncertain. A string of 30 balloons stretching across the sky in a wide circumference (whose centre, as in all 'pushes,' would have been somewhere behind our old front) industriously watched the enemy's back area. There was probably little comfort for the Germans west of Bapaume, or even in it, for our reluctance to shell towns, villages and (formerly most privileged of targets) churches was rapidly diminishing.

On November 21 the Brigade took over its new sector of the line and with it a somewhat different régime to what it had known before. It was heard said of the 61st Division that it stayed too long in quiet trenches (to be sure, trenches were only really 'quiet' to those who could afford to visit them at quiet periods). Still the Somme 'craterfield' presented a complete contrast to the old breastworks with their familiar landmarks and daylight reliefs. Battle conditions remained though the advance had stopped. Our recent capture of Beaumont-Hamel and St. Pierre Divion left local situations, which required clearing up. The fragments of newly-won trenches above Grandcourt, trenches without wire and facing a No-Man's-Land of indeterminate extent, gave their occupants their first genuine tactical problems and altogether more responsibility than before. In some respects the Germans were quicker than ourselves to adapt themselves to conditions approximating to open

THE SOMME BATTLEFIELD, NOVEMBER, 1916. 25

warfare. The principle of an outpost line and the system of holding our ,front in depth had been pronounced often as maxims on paper, but had resulted rarely in practice. Subordinate staffs, on whom the blame for local reverses was apt to fall rather heavily, were perhaps reluctant to jeopardise the actual front line by holding it too thinly, while from the nature of the case, the front line was something far more sacred to us than to the enemy. Since the commencement of trench warfare the Germans had held their line on the 'depth' principle, keeping only a minimum of troops, tritely referred to as 'caretakers,' in their front trench of all, while we for long afterwards crammed entire companies, with their headquarters, into the most forward positions.

On the evening of November 25, 1916, Robinson of C Company and myself, taking Hunt and Timms (my runner) and one signaller, left for the front line. This was being held along Desire—my fondness for this trench never warranted that name—with a line of resistance in Regina, a very famous German trench, for which there had recently been heavy fighting. Our reconnaissance, which was completed at dawn, was lucky and satisfactory; moreover—I do not refer to any lack of refreshment by the Berks company commander—I was still dry at its conclusion, having declined all the communication trenches, which were already threatening to become impassable owing to mud.

The next night the Battalion moved up to relieve the Berks, but was conducted, or conducted itself, along the very communication trench which

I had studiously avoided using and which was in a shocking state from water and mud. As the result of the journey, D Company reached the front line practically wet-through to a man, and in a very exhausted condition. A proportion of their impedimenta had become future salvage on the way up, while several men and, I fancy, some officers, had compromised themselves for some hours with the mud, which exacted their gumboots as the price of their future progress. I regret that my own faithful servant, Longford, was as exhausted as anybody and suffered a nasty fall at the very gates of paradise (an hyperbole I use to justify the end of such a mud-journey), namely Company Headquarters in Regina, where, like a sort of host, I had been waiting long.

Desire Trench, the name by which the front line was known, was a shallow disconnected trough upholstered in mud and possessing four or five unfinished dug-out shafts. These shafts, as was natural, faced the wrong way, but provided all the front line shelter in this sector. At one end, its left, the trench ran into chalk (as well as some chalk and plenty of mud into *it*!) and its flank disappeared, by a military conjuring trick, into the air. About 600 yards away the Germans were supposed to be consolidating, which meant that they were feverishly scraping, digging and fitting timbers in their next lot of dug-outs. To get below earth was their first consideration.

Regina dug-out deserves a paragraph to itself. This unsavoury residence housed two platoons of D Company, Company Headquarters, and Stobie, our doctor, with the Regimental Aid Post. In construction the dug-out, which indeed was typical of many, was a corridor with wings opening off, about 40 feet deep and some 30 yards long, with 4 entrances, on each of which stood double sentries day and night. Garbage and all the putrefying matter which had accumulated underfoot during German occupation and which it did not repay to disturb for fear of a worse thing, rendered vile the atmosphere within. Old German socks and shirts, used and half-used beer bottles, sacks of sprouting and rotting onions, vied with mud to cover the floor. A suspicion of other remains was not absent. The four shafts provided a species of ventilation, reminiscent of that encountered in London Tubes, but perpetual smoking, the fumes from the paraffin lamps that did duty for insufficient candles, and our mere breathing more than counterbalanced even the draughts and combined impressions, fit background for post-war nightmares, that time will hardly efface. Regina Trench itself, being on a forward slope and exposed to full view from Loupart Wood, was shelled almost continuously by day and also frequently at night. 'Out and away,' 'In and down' became mottoes for runners and all who inhabited the dug-out or were obliged to make repeated visits to it. Below, one was immune under 40 feet of chalk, and except when an entrance was hit the 5.9s rained down harmlessly and without comment.

During the day I occasionally ploughed my way along Regina Trench to some unshelled vantage point to watch the British shells falling on the yet grassy slopes above Miraumont and south of Puisieux. Baillescourt Farm was a very common target. At this time Miraumont village was comparatively intact and its church, until thrown down by our guns, a conspicuous object. Grandcourt lay hidden in the hollow.

Such landscape belonged to the days; real business, when one's orbit was confined to a few hundred yards of cratered surface, claimed the nights. A peculiar degree of darkness characterised these closing days of November, and with rain and mud put an end to active operations. Wiring, the chief labour of which was carrying the coils up to the front and afterwards settling the report to Brigade, occupied the energies of the Battalion after rations had been carried up. In this last respect much foresight and experience were required and arrangements were less good than they soon afterwards became; food that was intended to arrive hot arrived cold, and, having once been hot, received precedence over things originally cold but ultimately more essential. Hot-food containers proved too unwieldy for the forward area.[1]

Although quite a normal circumstance in itself, the extreme darkness at this period was a real obstacle to patrols and to all whose ability to find

[1] In making these remarks I want it understood that I am intending at this point no censure of our staff, whose difficulties in their way were even greater than those of the Infantry, nor am I working up to any impeachment of my superiors in narrating those facts, the omission of which would ruin the value of this story.

the way was their passport. Amid these difficulties there was an element of humour. To make one false turn, or to turn without noticing the fact, by night threw the best map-reader or scout off his path and bewildered his calculations. One night about this time a party of us, including Hunt and 'Doctor' Rockall, the medical corporal, who had accompanied me round the front posts, lost its way hopelessly in the dark. Shapes looming up in the distance, I enquired of Hunt as to his readiness for hostile encounter, whereupon the reassuring answer was given that 'his revolver was loaded, but not cocked.' I leave the point (if any) of this story to the mercy of those whose fate it has been to lose their way on a foggy night among shell-holes, broken-down wire and traps of all descriptions. Temporary bewilderment of the calculation destroyed reliance on any putative guides such as 'Verey' lights, shells, rifle fire, &c., which on these occasions appeared to come from all directions, and English and German seemed all alike.

Hunt, who at this time, being my only officer not partially sick, has called for somewhat repeated reference, usually devoted the hours after mid-night to taking a patrol to locate a track shown on the map and called Stump Road, his object being to meet another patrol from a neighbouring unit. Success did not crown the work. Stump Road remained undiscovered and passed into the apocrypha of trench warfare.

At 5 p.m on November 29, 1916, the Germans opened a heavy barrage with howitzers on the front line, giving every indication of impending attack.

Regina Trench, where were the headquarters of C and D, the companies then holding the line, was also heavily shelled, and telephonic communication with the rear was soon cut. On such occasions it was always difficult to decide whether or not to send up the S.O.S—on the one hand unnecessary appeal to our artillery to fire on S.O.S. lines was deprecated, on the other, no forward commander could afford to guess that a mere demonstration was on foot; for the appearance of attacking infantry followed immediately on a lifting of the barrage, a symptom in itself often difficult to recognise. On this occasion I intended and attempted to send up a coloured rocket, but its stick became stuck between the sides of the dug-out shaft and, by the time the efforts of Sergeant Collett had prepared the rocket for firing, the barrage died down as suddenly as it had started. This very commonplace episode illustrates the routine of this phase of warfare. The trenches were, of course, blown in and some Lewis guns damaged, but, as frequently, few casualties occurred.

While speaking of the life furthest forward I do not forget the very similar conditions, allowing for the absence of enemy machine-guns and snipers, which prevailed at Battalion Headquarters. Confined to a dug-out (a smaller replica of Regina) in Hessian Trench, with a continual stream of reports to receive and instructions to send out, and being continually rung up on the telephone, Colonel Bellamy and Cuthbert had their hands full, and opportunities for rest, if not for refreshment, were very limited. Nor do I omit our runners from the fullest share in the dangers and activities of this time.

Under battle-conditions life at one remove from the front line was rarely much more agreeable than in the line itself, and was less provided with those compensations which existed for the Infantryman near the enemy. It was necessary to go back to Divisional Headquarters to find any substantial difference or to live an ordered life on a civilised footing; and there, too, responsibility had increased by an even ratio.

The Battalion Transport during this time was stationed at Martinsart and its task, along bad roads, in bringing up rations each day was not a light one.

On the night of November 30 the Battalion was relieved by the 2/4th Gloucesters and marched back to huts in Martinsart Wood. This march of eight miles, coming after a four days' tour in wet trenches under conditions of open warfare, proved a trying experience. For four miles the path lay along a single duckboard track, capsized or slanting in many places, and the newly-made Nab Road, to which it led, was hardly better. A number of men fell from exhaustion, while others, their boots having worn completely through before entering the trenches, were in no state to compete with such a distance. After passing Wellington Huts and through Aveluy the going became easier, until at last the area of our big guns was reached and, adjoining it, the 'rest billets.' The latter consisted of unfloored huts built of tarred felt and surrounded by mud only less bad than in the trenches. Our lights and noise scared the rats, which infested the camp.

The relief and march occupied until 4 a.m., and were succeeded by mist and frost. The concussion of our neighbours, the 6-inch naval guns, echoed among the trees, heralding the first of December, 1916.

Chapter III.

CHRISTMAS ON THE SOMME,
December, 1916.

The move from Martinsart to Hedauville.—Back to Martinsart.—Working parties.—Dug-outs at Mouquet Farm.—Field Trench.—Return to the front line.—Getting touch.—Guides.—An historic patrol.—Christmas in the trenches.

ON December 2, 1916, the Battalion moved from Martinsart to Hedauville, on its way passing through Englebelmer, the home of one of our 15-inch howitzers, but no longer of its civilian inhabitants. The march was regulated by Pym, the new Brigade Major, who had replaced Gepp a few days before. The latter had proved himself a most efficient staff officer, and his departure to take up a higher appointment was regretted by everybody.

Hedauville was an indifferent village, but our billets were not bad. Brigade Headquarters were at the château. One heard much about the habitual occupation of the French châteaux by our staffs during the war. On this particular occasion the Brigade had only two or three rooms at its disposal, and on many others would be licencees of only a small portion of such buildings. The 184th Infantry Brigade Staff was always most solicitous about the comfort of battalions, and its efforts secured deserved appreciation from all ranks. During the winter Harling retired from the office of Staff Captain, and after a brief interregnum Bicknell, a Gloucester officer, who already had been attached to the Brigade for some time, received the appointment. For the ensuing three years Bicknell proved himself both an excellent staff officer and a consistent friend to the Infantry.

After scraping off the remains of the mud it had carried from the trenches, the Battalion settled down at Hedauville to a normal programme for ten days. The weather was bad, and a good deal of sickness now occurred among the troops, until so many officers were sick that leave for the others was stopped. Of general interest little occurred to mark this first fortnight of December. At its close the Battalion marched back to Martinsart and reoccupied its former huts. Battalion and Brigade were now in support, and our energies were daily devoted to working parties in the forward area. As these were some of the most arduous ever experienced by the Battalion I will describe an example.

I take December 16—a Saturday. My company was warned for working party last night, so at 6 a.m. we get up, dress, and, after a hurried breakfast, parade in semi-darkness. As the outing is not a popular one and reduction in numbers is resented by the R.E., the roll is called by Sergeant-Major Brooks (recently back from leave and in the best of early morning tempers) amid much coughing and scuffling about in the ranks. At 7 a.m.

we start our journey towards the scene of labour, some 80 strong (passing for 100). We go first along a broad-gauge railway line (forbidden to be used for foot traffic) and afterwards through Aveluy and past Crucifix Corner to near Mouquet Farm.

After a trivial delay of perhaps 40 minutes, the D.C.L.I. or 479 have observed our arrival and tools are counted out and issued, the homely pick and shovel. The task is pleasantly situated about 150 yards in front of several batteries of our field guns (which open fire directly we are in position) and consists in relaying duckboards, excavating the submerged sleepers of a light railway or digging the trench for a buried cable.

Perhaps the work only requires 50, not 100 (nor even 80) men. Very well! It is a pity those others came, but here are a thousand sandbags to fill, and there a pile of logs dumped in the wrong place last night, so let them get on with it!

For six hours we remain steadily winning the war in this manner and mildly wondering at the sense of things and whether the Germans will shell the batteries just behind our work—until, without hooter or whistle, the time to break off has arrived. By 3 p.m the party is threading its way back, and as darkness falls once more reaches the camp. Cries of 'Dinner up' and 'Tea up' resound through the huts, and all is eating and shouting.

By December 20 it was once more the Brigade's turn to relieve the front line. Berks and Gloucesters again took first innings in the trenches, while the Bucks and ourselves stayed in support. Battalion Headquarters with A and B Companies were in Wellington Huts, near Ovillers; C and D went two miles further forward to some scattered dug-outs between Thiepval and Mouquet Farm. My own headquarters were at the farm, to whose site a ruined cellar and a crumbling heap of bricks served to testify. The Germans had left a system of elaborate dug-outs, some of which now housed Brigade Headquarters, but others, owing to shelling and rain, had collapsed or were flooded. On each of the four nights spent at Mouquet Farm my company supplied parties to carry wire and stakes up to the front line. These journeys were made through heavy shelling, and we were always thankful to return safely. My policy was never to allow the pace to become that of the slowest man, for there was no limit to such slowness I myself set a pace, which I knew to be reasonable, and men who straggled interviewed me next day. By this policy the evening's work was completed in two-thirds of the time it would otherwise have taken, and my disregard of proverbial maxims probably saved the Battalion many casualties.

Since our last tour in the line real winter conditions had set in. Shell-holes and trenches everywhere filled with water till choice of movement was confined to a few duckboard tracks. Those in our area led past Tullock's Corner and from the Gravel Pit to Mouquet Farm, and thence to the head of Field Trench, with a branch sideways to Zollern Redoubt. Field Trench, an old German switch, led over the Pozières ridge, whose crest was well 'taped' by the German guns. The British advance having reached a standstill, the enemy's artillery was now firing from more forward positions and paid much attention to places like Mouquet Farm, Tullock's Corner, Zollern Redoubt and Field Trench. Parties of D.C.L.I. were daily at work

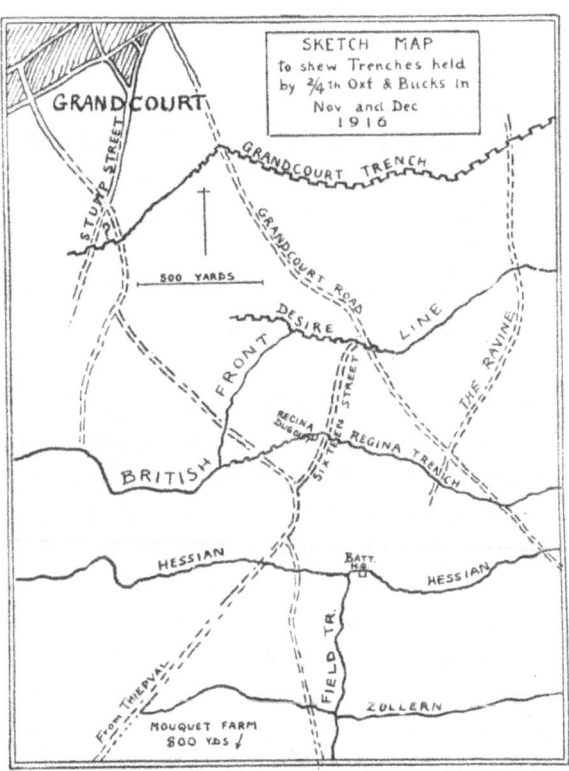

upon the latter, duckboarding and revetting, and completed a fine pioneers' job right up to Hessian. Field Trench ranked among the best performances of the Cornwalls, whose work altogether at this time deserved high praise.

On Christmas eve, 1916, the Battalion relieved the front line. Brown and Davenport took their companies to Desire and Regina. Battalion Headquarters had an improved position at Zollern Redoubt, and their old dug-out in Hessian was left to D Company Headquarters. Robinson with C Company was also in Hessian, to the left of D. His headquarters possessed plenty of depth but neither height nor breadth. The dug-out entrance was the size of a large letter-box and nearly level with the trench floor.

After the march up, the remainder of the night was devoted to the trying process of 'getting touch.' This meant finding the neighbouring sentry-posts on each flank—an important duty, for the Germans usually knew the date and sometimes the hour of our reliefs and the limits of frontage held by different units (we naturally were similarly informed about the enemy). For reasons of security no relief could be held complete before not only our own men were safely in but our flanks were established by touch with neighbouring posts.

In the course of the very relief I have mentioned, a platoon of one battalion reached the front line but remained lost for more than a day. It could neither get touch with others nor others with it. 'Getting touch' seemed easy on a map and was often done in statements over the telephone. Tangible relations were more difficult and efforts to obtain them often involved most exasperating situations, for whole nights could be spent meandering in search of positions, which in reality were only a few hundred yards distant. Total absence of guiding landmarks was freely remarked as the most striking chararteristic of this part of the Somme area. I refer only to night movement, for by day there were always distant objects to steer by, and the foreground, seemingly a cratered wilderness of mud, to the trained eye wore a multitude of significant objects.

My last topic introduces the regimental guide. Guides performed some of the hardest and most responsible work of the war. Staff work could at time be botched or boggled without ill-effects; for mistakes by guides some heavy penalty was paid. Whenever a relief took place, men to lead up the incoming unit into the positions it was to occupy were sent back, usually one per platoon, or, in cases of difficult relief and when platoon strengths were different, one per sentry-post. Guides rarely received much credit when reliefs went well, but always the blame when they went ill. The private soldiers, who guided our troops into trench and battle, played a greater part in winning the war than any record has ever confessed.

I have already spoken of patrols, their difficulties and dangers. Than General White no man in the Brigade was better acquainted with its front or a more punctual visitor to the most forward positions. What 'Bobbie' could not himself see by day he was resolved to have discovered for him by night, and thus a high measure of activity by our patrols was required. About Christmas the question whether the eastern portion of a trench, known as Grandcourt Trench, was held by the enemy, was set to the Battalion to answer. Vowed to accomplish this task or die, a picked patrol started one dark night. Striking in a bee line from our trenches, the patrol passed several strands of wire and presently discovered fragments of unoccupied trench. On further procedure, sounds were heard and, after the necessary stalking and listening, proof was obtained that a large hostile wiring party, talking and laughing together, was only a few yards distant. With this information the patrol veered to a flank, again passing through wire and crossing several trenches which bore signs of occupation. A line for home was then taken, but much groping and long search failed to reveal the faithful landmarks of our front line. At length, as dawn was breaking, the situation became clear. The patrol was outside D Company Headquarters in Hessian, more than 800 yards *behind* the front line. The report of German wiring parties laughing and talking did not gratify, and on reconstruction of its movements it was found that the patrol had spent the entire night reconnoitring not the German but our own defensive system. The wire so easily passed through, the noise and laughter, and the final *dénouement* at Hessian allowed for no other conclusion. A few nights later Brown, with a small party and on a clear frosty night, solved the riddle by boldly walking up to Grandcourt Trench and finding the Germans not at home.

I mention the story of this first patrol for the benefit, perhaps, of some who took part in it and who will now, I feel sure, enjoy the humour of its recollection. I mention it more to show of what unrequited labour Infantry was capable. The most

CHRISTMAS ON THE SOMME, DECEMBER, 1916.

wholehearted efforts were not always successful. One had this confidence on patrol, that one's mistakes only affected a handful. It was otherwise for artillery commanders who arranged a barrage, commanders of Field Companies who guaranteed destruction of a bridgehead, or of Special Companies undertaking a gas projection. Such was the meaning of responsibility.

The Battalion spent December 25, 1916, in the trenches under some of the worst conditions that even a war Christmas could bring. Christmas dinners were promised and afterwards held when we were in rest.

As in previous years, our army circulars had forbidden any fraternisation with the enemy. Though laughed at, these were resented by the Infantry in the line, who at this stage lacked either wish or intention to join hands with the German or lapse into a truce with him. On the other hand, a day's holiday from the interminable sounds of shelling would have been appreciated, and casualties on Christmas Day struck a note of tragedy. This want of sagacity on the part of our higher staff, as if our soldiers could not be trusted to fight or keep their end up as well on Christmas as any other day, was a reminder of those differences on which it is no object of this history to touch.

Chapter IV.

AT MAISON PONTHIEU,

January—February, 1917.

Visitors to the Battalion.—The New Year.—A wintry march.—Arrival at Maison Ponthieu.—Severe weather.—At war with the cold.—Training for offensive action.—By rail to Marcelçave.—Billets at Rainecourt.—Reconnoitring the French line near Deniécourt.

I CANNOT often treat my readers to a ride by motor car. Jump into this staff car that is waiting—it will not take you to the trenches! You will have distinguished company. Colonel A. and Major Q. have decided to pay a visit to the Battalion. It is at Maison Ponthieu, nearly 50 miles behind the line, whither it marched two days since to undergo a period of rest.

Arrived there, you learn that the Commanding Officer is out, placating with the assistance of the Brigade interpreter the wrath of the village hunchback, a portion of whose wood-stack was reported missing last night. This is not the first time that A. and Q. have visited the village (their lives are martyred to the study of regimental comfort), so our journey opens with an inspection of the two Nissen huts on the village 'green.'

'Disgraceful! At least two planks, which helped to line the roof of this hut, have been burnt. Stoves? One was sent to each battalion only yesterday, and ten more have been promised by Corps. Fuel? I am astounded to hear that the supply is inadequate. Quartermaster! How many pounds of dripping did you send to the Base last week? The A.S.C. sent twice that quantity. Who is cooking on that field kitchen? It will be impossible to make the war last if things are abused in this way. Your men have no rifle racks, more ablution benches must be provided and the sanitary arrangements made up to date . . . .'

This little parable has made me outstrip my narrative. You must come another day and see what Sergeant Parsons is doing with the vast quantities of timber, corrugated iron, and other stores supplied to make the billets staff-proof for the future.

The end of the last chapter left the Battalion complaining of our guns and otherwise merry-making in the front line. A day or two before the New Year, companies marched back to huts near Pioneer Station and the next morning reached Hedauville. Here, shortly afterwards, Christmas dinners, consisting of pigs and plum-pudding, were consumed. It was believed that we had left Regina and Desire for good, were leaving the Corps and likely to do training in a back area for several weeks. Colonel Bellamy went on leave, and Bennett, amid many offers to accompany him as batman, departed for three months' instruction at Aldershot as a senior officer. A new Major, W. L. Ruthven, arrived in January and temporarily was in command. Loewe and John Stockton returned from hospital and Jones from a Divisional working party, which had been engaged for a month on the wholesale manufacture of duck-boards. Lyon, an officer equally popular in and out of the line, had found egress from the Somme dug-outs troublesome and withdrew for a time to easier spheres. Men's leave was now going well and frequent parties left Acheux Station for 'Blighty.'

This list of changes is, of course, incomplete, and I only give it to show how constantly the wheel of alteration was turning. Comparatively few officers or men stayed very long with one battalion. 'Average lives' used to be quoted for all cases, ranging from a few weeks for a platoon officer to the duration for R.T.O's and quartermaster-sergeants! Old soldiers may never die, but I think our new soldiers 'faded away,' not the old, who grew fat and crafty!

The Battalion marched away from Pioneer Huts—whither it had returned after its rest at Hedauville—on January 15. The first stage on the rearward journey carried us to Puchevillers, a village full of shell dumps and now bisected by a new R.O.D. line from Candas to Colincamps. Snow, which had fallen heavily before we left Puchevillers, made the ensuing march through Beauval and Gézaincourt to Longuevillette a trying one. The going was quite slippery and the Transport experienced difficulty in keeping up with the Battalion, especially for the last two miles. The road marked on the map had by that time degenerated, in characteristic fashion, to a mere farm track across country. The Battalion was in its billets at Longuevillette by 6 o'clock, but blankets arrived so late that it was midnight before Hobbs could issue them. On the next day, January 18, the march was continued through Bernaville to Domqueur, a distance of 11 miles, on frost-bound roads. No man fell out. The 2/4th Oxfordshire and Buckinghamshire Light Infantry

MAISON PONTHIEU.

was one of the best marching battalions in France. On January 19 we reached the promised destination, Maison Ponthieu, of whose billets glowing accounts had been received; which, as often, were hardly realised.

At Maison Ponthieu the Battalion remained for nearly three weeks. Brigade Headquarters, the Machine-gun Company, and some A.S.C. were already in the village—ominous news for a billeting party.

Now much snow had already fallen throughout the countryside, and the weather since the New Year had been growing steadily more cold. In the middle of January, 1917, an iron frost seized Northern France till ponds were solid and the fields hard as steel. This spell, which lasted a month, was proclaimed by the villagers to be the coldest since 1890. As day succeeded day the sun still rose from a clear horizon upon a landscape sparkling with snow and icicles, and each evening sank in a veil of purple haze. Similar frost was experienced in England, but the wind swept keener across the flat plains of Ponthieu than over our own Midlands. This turn of the weather was a military surprise. It produced conditions novel in trench warfare. Severe cold was a commonplace, but now for three weeks and more the ground everywhere had been hard as concrete, digging and wiring were quite impossible, and movement in our front area easier than ever before. It almost seemed as if our opportunity for open warfare had arrived. Certainly at this moment in the military situation the enemy could not have availed himself of his old tactics as guarantee against a break through, nor could he, as formerly during the Somme Battle, have protected himself from gradual defeat by digging fresh trenches and switch lines and putting out new wire in rear wherever his front line was threatened. No doubt there were reasons prohibiting an attempt to rush the enemy on a grand scale from his precarious salient between Arras and

AT MAISON PONTHIEU, JANUARY—FEBRUARY, 1917.

Péronne other than fear of being 'let down' by the weather; though perhaps the latter consideration alone, from a Supply standpoint, constituted sufficient veto.

At all events the tactics of the Battalion were in quite another order. How to shave, how to wash, how to put on boots frozen hard during the night, above all, how to keep warm—these were the problems presented. I doubt if there was much washing in cold water before parade, and, as for shaving, I know a portion of the breakfast tea was often used for this purpose. Sponge and shaving brush froze stiff as matters of habit. To secure fuel provided constant occupation and frequent stumbling-blocks. On our arrival most rigid orders had been issued not to burn our neighbours' fences and I am able to say that the fences survived our stay. Temptation grew, nevertheless, in orchards and rows of small pollards (usually of ash), which formed the hedges in this part of France, not to mention a wood at the lower end of the village. That ancient trick of covering tree stumps with earth needed little learning. Each night for such as had ears, if not official ones, wood and thicket rang with the blows of entrenching tool on bole and sapling, till past the very door of Sergeant-Major sipping his rum, or company officers seated around sirloin and baked potatoes would be dragged trunk and branches of a young tree, that in peace time and warmer weather might have lived to grace an avenue. There should be variety in story telling; here was one told very much out of school.

From contemplation of this illicit forestry I pass to sterner matters. The first alarms of the 'spring offensive' were in the air, urging us infantry to deeds of arms in the back area. Pamphlets proclaimed the creed of open warfare and bade perish the thought of gumboot or of trench. Hence daily practices in attack formation, the following of barrages to first, second, and final objectives, the making of Z shaped posts and sending forward of patrols and scouts.

The Brigadier was an enthusiastic spectator of the work, and woe betide the platoon officer whose men gave reckless answers to the General's questions. The 'Platoon Test' was introduced.[1] Soldier's catechism did not yet reach the perfection it afterwards acquired, when all who took part in an attack knew beforehand every practical detail assigned to them. While knowledge of the complexities of the war became steadily more important, individual training of the man helped to make good his deficiency in pre-war discipline. Morale was never learnt from sack-stabbing at home, but in France this education of each soldier to use his intellect and become a positive agent instead of a member of a herd proved a potent

[1] Cross-examination of the men in their duties. They were asked what they would do in various emergencies. Their powers of recognition were also tested. I recollect a humorous incident when General White and Colonel Wake (G.S.O.I., 61st Division) both passed *incognito*. The situation was well seized by the former, who slapped his chest and declared, ' Such is fame ' ! Lay readers will find in later chapters some attempt to explain the technical expressions used in the text.

BRIGADIER-GENERAL THE HON. R. WHITE, C.B., C.M.G., D.S.O.

factor towards the final superiority of the Englishman over his enemy.

On the morning of February 4, 1917, the Battalion has said good-bye to Maison Ponthieu and is marching to Brucamps. Another week and we see it on the move again, this time partly by train. Orders for that move were as follows:—

>Reveille, 5 a.m.
>Breakfast, 6 a.m.
>Blankets rolled in tens and valises to be dumped outside the Q.M. stores by 6.30 a.m.
>Mess boxes, 7 a.m.
>Parade, 7.30 a.m.

The march was through Vauchelles-les-Domart to Longpré. Thence we were dragged by train through Amiens to Marcelçave, where we detrained and marched to huts at Wiencourt. We were about to relieve the French in the line near Chaulnes.

On February 15 the Battalion marched through Harbonnières, where the Major-General, Colin Mackenzie (now Sir Colin, K.C.B.) was standing with a French General to see us pass, and on to Rainecourt. The latter village, where the Battalion was billeted, improved on acquaintance. It had lain some 3½ miles behind the old Somme front and had suffered a good deal from German shells. French industry and French materials had, since the advance, converted damaged barns and houses into quite good billets.

Several days were spent in Rainecourt in rather dismal weather, for the prolonged frost had broken and mist and mud followed. Into the little church were now dragged 6,400 pairs of gumboots, representing about £10,000. It was the Divisional gumboot store, phrase of awful significance! I feel that the very mention of the word gumboot, when-

HARBONNIÉRES.

ever it occurs, is lending a smile to certain of my readers and, perchance, a frown to others. O gumboots, what reputations have you not jeopardised, what hairs brought down with sorrow to the Base!

The Battalion was divided before it left Rainecourt, orders being given for C and D Companies to move forward to Herleville and occupy some huts and dug-outs there.

* * * *

It is morning of February 22, 1917. Colonel Bellamy and his four company commanders are setting out to reconnoitre the new front line. Guides are to meet us at Deniécourt Château, a heap of chalk slabs and old bricks, beneath which are Brigade Headquarters. To reach this *rendezvous* we pass through Foucaucourt and then along a corduroy road through Deniécourt Wood to the village of that name. The wood has been fought through and but few branches remain on the trees, whose trunks, like so many untidy telegraph poles, rise to various heights from the upheaval of shell-holes and undergrowth. Dismal surroundings on a dismal morning, for the frost has relented for several days and already sides of trenches are collapsing (flop go the chunks into the water!) and on top the ground is loading one's boots at every step.

We change into gumboots in an old cellar and our journey commences. See the Colonel, Cuthbert, Marcon, Brown, Stockton, Robinson and myself lead off down a communication trench behind a guide, pledged to take us to the Berks Headquarters. The going is desperate—water up to our knees; however, each hundred yards brings our goal nearer, and it can hardly be like this all the way. We come to a trench junction, and our guide turns left-handed; presently another—the guide knows the way and again turns to the left.

Confound the mud! If we do not get there soon we shall never be home for lunch .... but we do not get there soon. The guide, always protesting that he knows the way, has led us in a circle and here we are whence we started an hour ago!

After such well-meaning mockery of our efforts, a route 'over the top' is tried. Soon we are outside Battalion Headquarters of the Berks. Whilst we are there, German gas shelling starts—a few rounds of phosgene—and helmets require to be adjusted. It is not everybody's helmet that fits, this being the first real occasion on which some officers have worn them. There is some laughing to see the strictest censor of a gas helmet (or its absence) in difficulties with his own, when the moment for its adjustment has arrived.

The company commanders duly separate to go up to their own sections of the front. They see the 'posts,' or any of them that can be visited in daylight, make notes of local details affecting the relief, and so home independently.

Billets never seemed so comfortable or attractive as on the night preceding a relief. Perhaps they would have seemed more so had the Battalion known, what luckily it could not, that an unpleasant tour was in store, and that afterwards, with the enemy in retreat, there would be no more billets until the summer.

Chapter V.

IN THE ABLAINCOURT SECTOR,

February, 1917.

German retreat foreshadowed.—The Battalion takes over the Ablaincourt Sector.—Issues in the making.—Lieutenant Fry mortally wounded.—The raid by German storm-troops on February 28.—The raid explained.

EARLY in 1917 it became known to our intelligence service that the enemy was contemplating retirement on a large scale from the Somme battle-front. Reports from prisoners and aeroplane photographs of a new line, famous afterwards as the Hindenburg line, running from west of Cambrai to St. Quentin, left in doubt only the date and manner of the withdrawal. To the latter question some answer was possible by reference to our mentors or from a text-book appreciation of the situation, though no one guessed until the movement had in reality started with what circumstances the Germans would see fit to invest it. The date was a more difficult problem. For its solution recourse must be had by commanders, staff officers and experts to the infantry A competition open to all battalions holding the line (and without other entrance fee) thereupon commenced. To whom should fall the laurels of a correct diagnosis of the march-table of the German rearguards, who be the first to scatter them by the relentless pursuit of our victorious arms?

To our higher staff the question whether the enemy was still manning with normal garrisons the front opposite our armies seemed relatively simple. Readers, however, with experience of trench warfare will remember that in the line by day it was impossible to surmise correctly one item of what was happening a hundred yards away in hostile trenches; certainly one knew well enough when shells were falling, and 'minnies,' rifle-grenades and snipers' bullets argued that a pernicious, almost verminous, form of life was extant not far away; but despite all this, stared a sentry never so vigilantly through his periscope he could hardly predict whether two, ten, or a hundred of the enemy tribe were hidden below earth almost within a stone's throw. At night it seemed probable that a patrol of a few brave men could crawl right up to the German wire and listen, or by setting foot in them enquire whether 'Fritz' was at home in his trenches or no; and so our patrols could, and did. In practice, however, our most active patrols were frequently deceived. Shots and Verey lights, which came from several directions, might be discharged by a solitary German, whose function it was to go the round of the enemy posts and fire from each spasmodically in turn. A trench entered and found empty might be a disused sap or bay habitually unoccupied. To maintain the normal semblance of trench-warfare was an easy task for the German, and one that he never failed in. Repeatedly in his retirements during the war he removed his real forces, his artillery and stores unbeknown to our watching infantry and their questioning staff. The screen of a retreating enemy is not easily caught up and pierced by an advanced guard not superior to it in strength and inferior in mobility. On the Somme in 1917 and from the Lys salient in 1918 the Germans retired from wide to narrower divisional fronts (giving themselves greater 'depth' in the process), which fact, coupled with destruction of bridges and roads, prevented us from forcing an issue with their main body on the move. There were exceptions, as when the 32nd Division captured guns near Savy, but the enemy, in retiring, played for safety and denied much opportunity to our troops, despite their zeal in keeping touch, to deal him damage.

Such was the tactical situation when the 184th Infantry Brigade relieved the French in the Ablaincourt sector. The Berks, who first held the left subsector, had an uneventful tour. Trenches taken over from the French were usually quiet at first owing to the different methods employed by us and our allies in the conduct of trench-warfare. Within a day or two of the relief the frost had finally broken and the trenches everywhere started to fall in, making the outlook in this respect ominous.

On the afternoon of February 23, we marched up to relieve the Berks. Near Foucaucourt the cookers gave us tea. There also we changed into gumboots. Guides met us at Estrées cross-roads, a trysting place possible only when dusk had fallen, and the lugubrious procession started along a tramway track among whose iron sleepers the men floundered considerably, partly from their precaution of choosing gumboots several sizes too large. On this occasion the usual stoppages and checks were multiplied by a brisk artillery 'strafe' upon the front, accompanied by all manner of coloured lights and rockets. The noise soon dying down we were able to continue a bad journey with men frequently becoming stuck and a few lost. The relief was not over until nearly dawn, by when the last Berks had left and our worst stragglers been collected.

The Battalion took over a three-company front. Brown with A Company guarded the left. Robinson with C (containing a large proportion of a recent draft now paying its first visit to the trenches) was in the centre, and D Company on the right. Some 500 yards behind our front lay the Ablaincourt Sucrerie, a dismal heap of polluted ruins, like all sugar factories the site of desperate fighting. Ablaincourt itself, a village freely mentioned in French dispatches during the Somme battle, was the very symbol of depressing desolation. Péronne, eight miles to the north-east, was out of view. Save for the low ridge of Chaulnes, whence the German gunners watched, and the shattered barn-roofs of Marchélepot—the former on our right, the latter directly to our front—the scene was mud, always mud, stretching appallingly to the horizon.

* * * * *

Students of music are familiar with the rival motifs that run through operas. In an earlier paragraph I have indicated one such motif, and if

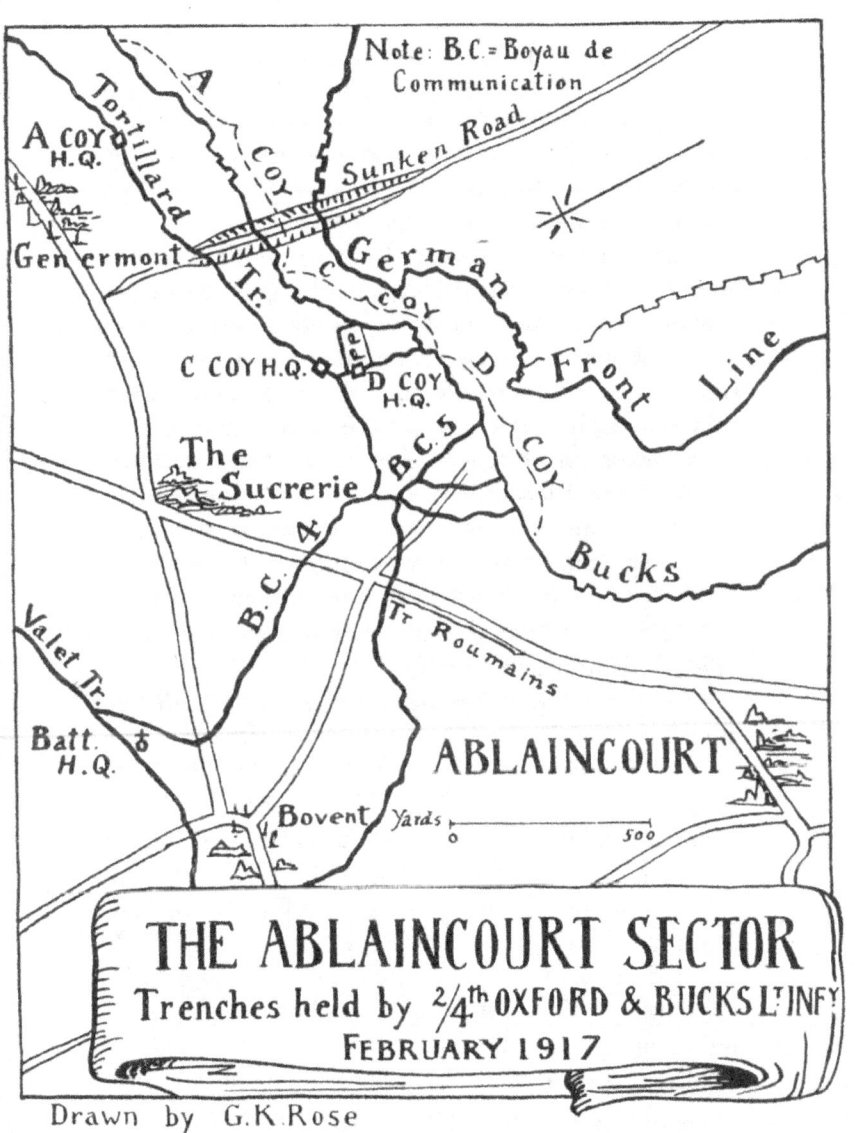

in this opera of war a curtain be lifted to shew the future act which this motif dominates, you would see the German staff busy with maps over its retreat, planning the time-table of explosion and burning, and designating the several duties of fouling wells and laying booby-traps.

Another scene, in which the rival motif is heard, shews a strong body of ugly-looking Germans at practice over some shallow trenches some distance behind their line. By a quaint coincidence these trenches are a facsimile of those just taken over by the Battalion. The ugly Germans are members of a 'travelling circus.' For long past they have lived in the best billets and been receiving extra rations. They play no part in the retreat—house-wrecking, the flooding of cellars, the hacking through of young fruit trees and throwing over of sundials and garden ornaments, much as they might enjoy it, is not their function.

They are a professional raiding party, with two successful raids at Loos, one at Ypres and one near Hébuterne to their credit. Wherever the English have just relieved the French they are sent for to perform. They are accompanied by two 8-inch howitzers and several batteries of 5·9s and 4·2s belonging to the 'circus' and by a Minen-Werfer Abteilung. Their raid upon the Oxfords is fixed for February 28, when the moon will be a third full. The last aeroplane photograph admirably shews the Sucrerie, communication trenches leading forward and the whereabouts of all dug-outs. The pioneer detachment—whose thoughts are turned only to the retreat, of which rumours have been plentiful—must move from its comfortable dug-outs in the railway embankment to make room for H.Q. of the raiding party.

* * * *

The front held by the Battalion was tactically not satisfactory. Being three on a front, with B Company placed nearly 1,000 yards in rear, companies had to find their own supports, which, owing to absence of other dug-out accommodation, were disposed in positions not only too far back but inadequately covering those portions of the front which they were engaged to defend. Moreover, practical means of communication to and by these support platoons were likely to prove, in event of need, negligible. They were, in fact, isolated in places themselves not defensible and equally remote from company and battalion commanders. This situation was bad enough as *point d'appui* for an advance; to resist a counter-attack or raid it was deplorable. Like many similar situations, it was due to the lack of habitable trenches on the ground that should have been occupied and defended. It could be no one's fault either high up or low down that the line was held in this way, though perhaps had fewer men been allowed to crowd into trenches and dug-outs in the forward line, casualties in killed and prisoners might have been spared to the Battalion.

A few hours after the relief was complete orders came up for patrols to go out to see if the enemy had or had not gone back yet. Our artillery, which was not yet strongly represented behind this sector, also began to fire at extreme ranges on the German

60 THE ABLAINCOURT SECTOR, FEBRUARY, 1917.

back area east of Marchélepot and Chaulnes. The enemy, on his part, sniped at and bombed our patrols at night. The behaviour of his guns and aeroplanes by day suggested no passive retreat in the near future. While BAB[1] code messages, providing mingled toil and excitement, announced the impending departure of the enemy and asserted the necessity for keeping touch, aeroplanes flew a thousand feet overhead and directed the fire of fresh batteries of 5·9s and 4·2s upon our trenches. No doubt the Germans had stocks of ammunition they preferred to fire off rather than cart backwards. Gas shelling became common for the first time in the Battalion's experience. In the front line masks had often to be worn. Headquarters also were gassed more than once and suffered much inconvenience. This activity by the enemy was reasonably regarded as his normal policy with which to impede our preparations for advance, so that complaints of registration[2] coming from the front line received no special attention from the authorities, who were themselves tossed to and fro and kept quite occupied by the many conflicting prophecies of the enemy's retreat.

On the morning of February 27 German howitzer batteries commenced some heavy shelling on the Battalion sector, especially on the communication trenches passing under the former French titles of B.C.4 and B.C.5.[3] Working parties who

---

[1] A secret trench code, intended for use in operations.

[2] Deliberate shelling to ascertain exact range of targets for a future bombardment.

[3] B.C. = *Boyau de communicatione,* communication trench.

were busy digging out mud from those trenches were compelled to desist. At 10 o'clock I heard that Fry, the commander of No. 16 Platoon, had been hit by shrapnel on his way from Company H.Q. to the Sucrerie. To get him to the nearest shelter (C Company H.Q.) was difficult through the mud, and uncomfortable enough with 5·9s coming down close to the trench, but the men, as always, played up splendidly to assist a comrade. Soon afterwards, the doctor, in answer to a telephonic summons, appeared at my H.Q. On our way to reach Fry we were both knocked down in the trench by a 4·2, which also wounded Corporal Rockall in the shoulder-blade. I regret that Fry, though safely moved from the trenches the same night, had received a mortal wound. In him died a fine example of the platoon officer. He met his wound in the course of a trivial duty which, had I guessed that he would do it under heavy shelling, I should have forbidden him to undertake. His type of bravery, though it wears no decorations, is distinguished, more than all other, by the unwritten admiration of the Infantry

During that night I had a peculiar and interesting task. It was to report on the condition of all roads leading through our front line across No-Man's-Land. Mud, battle and frost had so combined to disguise all former roads and tracks, that to decide their whereabouts it was often necessary to follow them forward from behind by means of map and compass. Seen by pale moonlight, these derelict roads, in places pitted with huge craters or flanked by shattered trees, wore a mysterious charm. More eloquent of catastrophe than those thrown down by gale or struck by lightning are trees which shells have hit direct and sent, splintered, in headlong crash from the ranks of an avenue. If wood and earth could speak, what tales the sunken roads of France could find to tell!

Morning and afternoon of the next day, February 28, were fine and ominously quiet. Excessive quietness was often no good sign. Presentiments could have been justified. At 4.15 p.m. a strong barrage of trench mortars and rifle grenades began to beat upon the front line, accompanied by heavy artillery fire against communication and support trenches and the back area. This sequel to the previous registration clearly indicated some form of attack by the enemy. The rhythmic pounding of the heavy howitzers, whose shells were arriving with the regular persistency of a barrage table, suggested that a long bombardment, probably until after dusk, was intended. Under such circumstances it was the part of the Company Commander to 'stand to' and await events with the utmost vigilance. This never meant that the men should be ordered out into the trenches and the fire-steps manned, for to do so would have invited heavy casualties and demoralised the garrison before the opportunity for active resistance had arrived. To keep look-out by sentries, to watch for any lifting in the barrage, and to maintain communication with H.Q. and with the flanks were the measures required. Otherwise, except to destroy maps and papers, there was nothing to do but wait, for only in the most clumsily organised shows did the other side know zero. On this occasion, at the moment the German raiding party came over, a patrol consisting of Corporal Coles and Timms had only just returned from D Company front line. They said that though the shelling was heavy immediately behind and on the flanks, the wire was intact and there was no sign of attack. At dusk, therefore, there was nothing save the heavy shelling to report to Cuthbert over my telephone, which by luck held until cut by German wire-cutters.

Within a few minutes, shouts and a few rifle shots were heard, and the next moment bombs were being thrown into my dug-out.

The lights went out and the interior became filled with fumes, groans, and confusion.

A German raiding party had penetrated C Company, seized the front line, which was a bare 80 yards from my H.Q., and, without touching my own front (which indeed was 200 yards distant and to the flank), had picketed my dug-out, and awaited their haul of prisoners.

Now, a bombed dug-out is the last word in 'unhealthiness.' It ranks next to a rammed submarine or burning aeroplane. For several minutes I awaited death or wounds with a degree of certainty no soldier ever felt in an attack. But in such emergencies instinct, which, more than the artificial training of the mind, asserts itself, arms human beings with a natural cunning for which civilization provides no scope. Life proverbially is not cheap to its owner.

That everyone inside was not killed instantly was due, no doubt, both to the sloping character of the stairs, which made some bombs explode before they reached the bottom, and to the small size of the bombs themselves. A gas bomb finished the German side of the argument. Hunt's useful knowledge of German commenced the answer. We 'surrendered.' I went upstairs at once and saw three Germans almost at touching distance. In place of a docile prisoner they received four revolver shots, after which I left as soon as possible under a shower of bombs and liquid fire. Shortly afterwards, but too late to follow me, Hunt also came forth and found the enemy had vanished Afterwards the Sergeant Major and Uzzell, sanitary lance-corporal, who on this occasion showed the genius of a field marshal, emerged and prevented the return of our late visitors.

After an hour's struggle through mud and barrage I reached the two platoons in Trench Roumains, who (I mention this as a good paradox of trench discipline) were engaged in sock-changing and foot-rubbing according to time table! From there the counter-attack described in Sir Douglas Haig's dispatch of March 1st was carried out. I fear this 'counter-attack' was better in his telling than in the doing, for the Germans had already decamped an hour before, taking with them Lieutenant Guildford and some 20 prisoners from C Company, several Lewis guns, and their own casualties.

Against a front line crowded with untried

troops (I refer to the new draft of which the platoons holding C Company front line were principally composed) a well-planned raid powerfully pressed home under a severe box barrage and assisted by gas and liquid fire, was almost bound to succeed. The mud, strange trenches and weak artillery support were other factors for which allowance might have been made before such degree of blame was laid upon the Battalion as was seen fit for it to receive. The only cure for being raided is to raid back. That was happily done exactly two months later against the very regiment to which the German raiding party on this occasion belonged. Nor was it true that the enemy was not fought with. Some parties which attacked Brown's front were, under the able example of that officer, driven off with Lewis guns, and D Company, whose loss in prisoners was nil, also maintained its front intact. Casualties were inflicted on the enemy, but these mostly regained their own lines or were carried back by stretcher parties. Our loss in killed that night amounted to some twenty.

The story of this raid I should not have allowed to reach this length but for the fact that the affair created some stir at the time, and correspondence raged on the subject till long afterwards Hunt, who was with me during the bombardment and the bombing of my H.Q., was not captured on emerging from the dug-out; but himself, some hour or more afterwards, while wandering among the blown-in trenches in an effort to follow me, entered a German listening post and became a prisoner. As a prisoner he was present at a German H.Q.

when the details of an exactly similar raid upon a neighbouring division were being arranged; which raid proved for the enemy an equal success.

The aftermath of this fighting proved a trying experience. The dug-out to which I returned to spend the remainder of the tour was a shambles. The stairs were drenched with blood. Of my companions, Thompson, a signaller, Timms, Smith (Hunt's servant, a fine lad) and Corporal Coles—one of the bravest and most devoted N.C.O.'s the Battalion ever had—were dead or died soon afterwards. Longford and Bugler Wright were severely wounded. Longley and Short had escaped before the first bombs exploded in the dug-out, but the remaining survivors, the Sergeant-Major, Lance Corporal Rowbotham, Roberts and myself were all partially gassed and hardly responsible for further action. Under these circumstances the task of carrying-on involved a strain, lessened, as always on such occasions, by management of everything for the best by Battalion Headquarters.

On the night of March 2 the Battalion was relieved by the Berks, now under the command of Colonel Beaman, and moved back about 2,000 yards to some support trenches near Bovent Copse. From here companies were employed ration-carrying to the front line and cleaning the trenches. Considerable activity continued to be displayed by the German artillery and aeroplanes, in each of which respect we lacked superiority.

The enemy retreat appeared postponed or cancelled.

Chapter VI.

LIFE IN THE FRONT LINE,

Winter, 1916—1917.

Ignorance of civilians and non-combatants.—The front line posts.—Hardships and dangers.—Support platoons.—The Company Officers.—The Battalion relieved by the 182nd Brigade.

SO far I have said little of the hardships suffered by the Infantry. Indeed, in places I have laughed at them. Those scenes and experiences which marked a soldier's life in the front line will have been supplied by those who knew them as familiar background to my story. But I grudge leaving them to the imagination of civilian and non-combatant readers. I seriously doubt whether the average man or woman has the least inkling of what really happened 'out there.' Talk overheard or stories listened to may in special instances have revealed a fragment of the truth. For most people the lack of real perception was filled in by a set of catchwords. As the war dragged on, the civilian mind of England passed into a conventional acceptance of phrases habitually read but improperly understood, until the words 'raids,' 'barrages,' 'objective,' 'craters,' 'counter-attack,' 'consolidation,' became tolerated as everyday commonplaces. Take a war-despatch of 1916 or 1917—it is made up of a series of catch words and symbols. Plenty of our famous men, I am sure, who went to the front and perhaps wrote books afterwards, on arrival there made remarks no less foolish (and excusable) than the old lady's 'nasty slippery place' where Nelson fell. The Somme and Ypres battlefields are inconceivable by anyone who has seen nothing but the normal surface of the earth. The destruction of towns, villages and farms is without parallel in history or fiction. To witness some scenes in the Retreat of 1918 was to stake one's sanity. There are no standards by which civilians and non-combatants can appreciate the true facts of the war. Deliberate reproduction would hardly be believed. Suppose, for instance, this winter I were to dig a large hole in a field, a quarter fill it with liquid mud, and then invite four or five comrades, all arrayed in much warlike impedimenta, but lacking more extra covering than a waterproof sheet each, to the hole to spend two nights and a day in it—I should be credited with lunacy. Yet I should be offering a fair sample of front-line accommodation during the Great War.

Reliefs took place at night. Alike through snow or rain, or in a biting wind, the Infantry marched up from huts or ruined barns (its rest billets) to reach the line—a distance normally of seven miles. First by road, next by a slippery track, finally through a communication trench deep in mud, our soldiers had to carry each his rifle and 120 round of ammunition, a share of rations, gum-

A Front Line Post

LIFE IN THE FRONT LINE, WINTER, 1916—1917.

boots, a leather jerkin and several extras—a load whose weight was fully 50 pounds. Many staggered and fell. All finished the journey smothered in dirt. Boots, puttees and even trousers were sometimes stripped from the men by the mere suction of the mud, in which it was not unusual to remain stuck for several hours. Men, though not of our Battalion, were even drowned.[1]

Parties were often shelled on the way up, or else were lost and wandered far. From Headquarters, reached about midnight, of the Company being relieved guides would take two platoons into the front line 'posts,' the other two to the positions in support.

In the front line itself there was often no better shelter than an old tarpaulin or sheet of corrugated iron stretched across the trench. At some 'posts' there was nothing better to sit on than the muddy 'fire-step' or at best half a duck-board or an old bomb box. Despite continuous efforts to keep one dry place to stand, the floor was several inches deep in water and mud.

Movement in any direction, save for a few yards to the flanks if the mud had been cleared away or dammed up, in daylight was impossible. No visitors came by day. Stretcher bearers were not always near. A fire could not, or if it could, might not be lighted. Therefore no hot meal, except perhaps a little tea made over a 'Tommy's Cooker,' was procurable by day.

---

[1] This fact, which will hardly be credited by future generations, is related from the actual knowledge of the writer.

The post would be shelled or trench-mortared at intervals. In earlier days it might be totally blown up by a mine, or in later times bombed or machine-gunned from the air. For 30 to 40 high explosive shells to fall all round a post was quite common. Sometimes a 'dud' would fall inside it, or a huge 'Minnie,' which burst in the wire, cover the occupants with earth and splinters. The crash of these huge trench-mortar bombs was satanic; and there was always a next one to be waited for. Sometimes whole posts were wiped out. If there were wounded they could expect no doctor's help before night. Often by day, owing to mud and German snipers, it was impossible to lift a wounded man from where he had fallen.

Night, longer than day, was also worse. Pitch darkness, accompanied maybe by snow or mist, increased the strain. With luck the great compensation of hot food—tea and stew—would be brought up by the ration parties. But sometimes they were hit and were often lost and arrived several hours late. The sandbags containing a platoon's rations for a day were liable to be dropped, and bread arrived soaked through or broken and mud-stained. Moreover, the darkness which permitted parties from behind to reach the post also decreed that the post should get about its work. Had the wire a weak place, the Germans knew of it, and directly the wiring party set about mending it lights were sent up, which fell in the wire close to our men, and machine-gun bullets banged through the air. Besides the wire the parapet required constant attention. At one place, where a member of the post had been killed by a sniper, it would want building up; at another, a shell perhaps had dropped only a yard short of the trench during the evening 'strafe,' the passage would be blocked and the post's bomb-store buried. All this had to be put right before dawn. During the night a patrol would be ordered to go out. Men who were sentries by day or were the covering party for the wiring might be detailed for this. After that was over the same men took turns as sentries.

Sleep was confined to what those not on duty could snatch, wrapped only in the extra covering of a waterproof sheet, in a sitting posture on the firestep. At dawn, when the men at last could have slept heavily, came morning stand-to. This meant standing and shivering for an hour whilst it grew light and attempting to clean a mud-clogged rifle. Those Englishmen in England (and in France) who have slept warm in their beds throughout the war should remind themselves of those thousands of our soldiers who wet through, sleepless, fed on food which, served as it finally was up in the trenches, would hardly have tempted a dog, have stood watching rain-sodden darkness of night yield to dismal shell-bringing dawn, and have witnessed the monotonous routine of war till sun, earth, sky and all the elements of nature seemed pledged in one conspiracy of hardship.

What of the two platoons in 'support'?

Their lot was preferable. They were placed about 400 yards behind the actual front and lived (if such existed) in deep mined dug-outs. Until the later stages of the war deep dug-outs, which were subterranean chambers about 25 feet below the level of the ground and nearly shell-proof, were made only by the Germans, whose industry in this respect was remarkable. Found and inhabited by us in captured territory, these dug-outs had the defect that their entrances 'faced the wrong way,' *i.e.*, towards the German howitzers. Sometimes a shell, whose angle of descent coincided with the slope of the stairs, burst at the bottom of a dug-out, and then, of course, its occupants were killed. If no deep dug-outs were available, the support platoons lived in niches cut into the side of the trench and roofed over with corrugated iron, timber and sandbags. Such shelters afforded little protection against shelling.

In event of attack by the enemy it was the normal duty of support platoons to garrison a line of defence known as the 'line of resistance.' They might be ordered to make a counter-attack. When no fighting was taking place their work was likely to consist in carrying up rations and R.E. materials (wooden pickets, sandbags, coils of barbed wire, etc.) to the front line. This work had to be done at night, because in winter 'communication trenches' (which alone made daylight movement possible from place to place in the forward zone) were so choked with mud as to be impassable. The day was spent in 'mud-slinging,' *i.e.*, digging out falls of earth from the trench, rebuilding dug-outs or laying fresh duckboards (wooden slats to walk on in the trenches). When the evening's 'carrying parties' were finished, the men had some sleep, but

A DUCKBOARDED COMMUNICATION TRENCH

support troops were often used as night patrols in No-Man's-Land or as wiring parties.

After a day or longer in support they were sent up to relieve, *i.e.*, exchange positions with, their comrades in the front line posts. Four days was the usual 'tour' for a company. During it each platoon did two spells of 24 hours in the posts and the same back in support. When the four days were over, a fresh company relieved that whose tour was finished. The one relieved moved back to better conditions, but would still be in trenches and dug-outs until the whole Battalion was relieved.

The English infantryman stands for all ages as the ensample of heroic patience, which words or cartoon fail utterly to convey.

How did the Company Commander and his officers fare in the trenches?

The Platoon Officer shared every hardship with his 25 men. If there was a roofed-in hole with a box for a table he had it, for his messages were many. To the Company Commander a rough table was quite indispensable, and so were light and some protection from the rain. Without these essentials he could never have received nor sent his written instructions, consulted his maps nor spoken by telephone, on which he relied to get help from the artillery. The Company Sergeant-Major, a few signallers and some runners were his familiars, and he lived with and among these faithful men. Quite often the Company Commander's dug-out was appreciably the best in the company area. Sometimes it was little better than the worst. In the spring of 1918 it was often only a hole.

Every good Company Commander made a point of visiting each night all his front line posts and spending some time with each, not only to give orders, direct the work and test the vigilance of the sentries, but in order to keep up the Company's morale. The worse the weather or the shelling the higher that duty was. Likewise the Battalion Commander used to visit Company Headquarters once a day and every front line post at least once during a tour. The journey to the front line, possible only in darkness, was very dangerous. Shells were bound to fall at some point on the way, the enemy's machine guns or 'fixed rifles' were trained on every probable approach, and the Captain in ordinary trench warfare was as liable to be killed as any Private. Responsibility, however, made these nightly walks not only necessary but almost desirable.

To conditions such as I have described the Battalion returned to do another tour in the Ablaincourt sector. The line was again held by A on the left (owing to the former three-company system no proper interchange had been possible) and by B on the right. Davenport went to my old headquarters, which the enemy was now busy trench-mortaring, and held half the front previously held by C, which, with D Company, was now in support. To the usual evils were now added rifle-grenades filled with gas, which caused several casualties in A Company. D Company lost a good man in Lance Corporal Tremellen, who was wounded by a bullet through the legs when leading a ration party 'across the top,' and other N.C.O.'s went sick with trench fever. During this tour the energy of Corporal Viggers, of my company, was most remarkable. He did the work of ten.

On the night of March 15 the Brigade was relieved by the Warwicks. The Battalion moved back to Framerville, where Quartermaster's Stores and Transport rejoined.

Chapter VII.

THE ADVANCE TO ST. QUENTIN,

March to April, 1917.

The enemy's retirement.—Road-mending in No-Man's-Land.—The devastated area.—Open warfare.—The Montolu campaign.—Operations on the Omignon river.—The 61st Division relieved before St. Quentin.—End of trench-warfare.

ON March 16, 1917, the Germans left their front line and scuttled back behind the Somme.

The news of this threw everything into a miniature ferment. The Berks stopped practising a raid which they were to do on the Brigade's return to the old trenches. The General rode off apace. After orders and counter-orders the 2/4th marched dramatically to a map reference near Lihons and commenced pulling logs out of old French dug-outs. Much good work was done, but I believe the logs were never used. On the next day German aeroplanes saw the Battalion parade at X 17 c 3. 8. and march to its old billets at Rainecourt. Never was the old song 'Here we are again' more heartily rendered.

Meanwhile Divisional Headquarters advanced and seized a colony of dug-outs at Vermandovillers. Great eagerness was shown by everyone to see what the enemy had left behind and whither he had gone. Often during the advance parties of Infantry detailed to clear a village found members of a Royal Corps already in possession. In this race of the curious we were severely handicapped, for it had fallen to the 182nd Brigade to be the Advanced Guard of the 61st Division and to the 184th to follow in reserve. To us the task of roadmaking in No-Man's-Land was assigned. This proved quite interesting work. Except where shells had fallen on them or trenches been dug through, the roads, when once the mud had been removed, were found virtually intact. Soon G.S. wagons and limbers and 18-pounders were passing forward. The war was on the move.

To explore the former German trenches was a pleasing novelty. The front line was deep and fairly dry. Elbow marks at every 50 yards or so and bombs with caps screwed off vouched for the situation of old sentry posts. Communication trenches were derelict, nor did proper support nor second lines exist. The enemy's defence had been the merest shell.

The Battalion moved to Chaulnes on March 22. That village, damaged by our artillery, had been finally wrecked by the departing enemy, whose rude notices were scrawled on any walls still standing. 'One million tons of English shipping sunk in the month of February,' said one more polite than others. In spite of all that the Germans had done, quite good accommodation was found for all ranks, and its improvement by old doors, shutters, and selected *débris* from other ruins provided much amusement. Father Buggins and the Doctor, with a wheelbarrow, were to the fore collecting armchairs covered in red velvet. Stoves and fuel were abundant, and at this time booby-traps were few.

March 23 was spent in road mending between Vermandovillers and Chaulnes. An example of how surely organisation wins wars was there provided. We, who had come from Chaulnes, to work near Chaulnes were sent to fetch our tools from Vermandovillers. In fetching them we passed a company of Devons, employed on similar work at Vermandovillers, who were fetching their tools from Chaulnes—an episode fit for a war-pageant.

On the same afternoon we marched to Marchélepot. German sign-posts, old gun positions and burnt dug-outs were objects of interest on the way. Though cold, the weather was fine. Freedom from shelling was a treat. We moved again on March 25, when the Bucks arrived to take over our quarters at Marchélepot. Passing St. Christ, where the R.E. had bridged the Somme, we saw the first samples of German back-area demolition. At Ennemain the first big road-crater held up the Transport. Our destination, Athies, formerly a flourishing little town but since utterly wrecked and still smouldering, it was quite difficult to reach. Sent on ahead as member of a billeting party, I had to cross the Omignon river by a single plank thrown across a weir. Until they are blown up one rather forgets the blessing of bridges.

In Athies good enough quarters in cellars and half-basements were found for all. Headquarters went into the only roofed house in the town—and afterwards questioned their own wisdom. The house had been foreman's shed to a large factory, had been a Boche canteen, and, finally, the billet of the wrecking party. Though our advanced troops were in touch with the enemy some seven miles away in front, we were made to hold an outpost line each night east of the town. To bring up rations the Transport had all the distance from Framerville to cover—about eighteen miles. Never had Abraham so long a journey for this purpose.

The wanton mischief, now manifest everywhere that the advance carried us, became a favourite topic for correspondents from the front, but cannot be passed over without some record here. To us Infantry this advance was a sort of holiday from the real war. It was like going behind the scenes at a pantomime and discovering the secrets of the giant's make-up. No list of things destroyed could lend any conception of the wholesale massacre by the Germans of all objects both natural and artificial. Château and cottage, tree and sapling, factory and summer-house, mill race and goldfish pond were victims equally of their madness. Hardly the most trivial article had been spared. The completeness of the work astonished. Yet withal our discomfort was slight. It was the French civilians, whose lives and homes had been thus ruined, that such Prussian methods touched.

Amid this wreckage signs were perceptible of the enemy's weakening morale. Villages in no wise organised for defence and so remote from the German front as to have been outside the range of our furthest gun-fire, inevitably contained deep dugouts. Such precautions surpassed all prudence and were sufficient almost to argue lack of mental balance. Germans seemed crazy on dug-outs.

To resume the war. On March 30 the Warwicks entered Soyécourt and shortly afterwards the Bucks relieved their outpost line. We ourselves reached Tertry on the 30th, and the next night made bivouacs at Caulaincourt Château, formerly German Corps Headquarters, now wrecked past recognition. Amid the rubbish, whose heaps represented buildings of grace and dignity, the eye caught the half of a gigantic Easter egg. During our stay a German High Velocity gun several times shelled the château grounds. Our own artillery was now getting to work and made the nights lively with noise and flashes.

At 3 a.m. on April 1 C and D Companies were ordered forward to support the Bucks in an attack on the line of single railway which runs northwards from Vermand. The attack gained the ridge east of the railway and no support by us was wanted. Ten prisoners were captured by the Bucks, whose only casualties resulted from our own shells dropping short and an unfortunate mistake of some other troops, who lost direction and, pressing forward, encountered men of their own side. Towards evening the General ordered D Company forward to occupy Montolu Wood. The journey was made at dusk through a blinding storm of hail and rain. The wood to which I went was the wrong one altogether. Nevertheless to my wood my company returned twice later, till tactical recognition was gained for it from the failure of the staff to observe the mistake and my own to disclose it. The wood I went to was some half-mile distant from the proper one, but the same shape, as near the railway, and answering the General's map-description to a nicety. I like to think of my wood, where I was so rarely found, whither perplexed runners brought orders so late, where I never was relieved, but where my old shelters of tin and brushwood escaped disturbance in my absence.

At midnight, April 3/4, the Battalion relieved the Bucks. B, C, and D Companies shared the new outpost line. Headquarters and A Company went to Soyécourt. The relief, the first of its kind, was difficult. In my own front a small brushwood copse was reputed to contain a sentry post. The ground was dotted with small copses which the darkness made indistinguishable, and no report of this post's relief was ever made. When dawn was breaking in the sky, Sergeant Watkins, accompanied by the Bucks guides, returned to say that no sentry group nor post in any copse could be found. The most likely copse was then garrisoned and the night's mystery and labour ceased.

Further advance was evidently in store. The smoke of burning villages still mounted the sky. At night a glow showed where a great fire in St. Quentin was ablaze. The weather now changed for the worse. Hail, rain and snow prevailed alternately. A fierce wind blew. Winter conditions were repeated in the outpost line, where no shelter other than tarpaulins rigged across the shallow trenches existed. Nor was the artillery inactive.

As the enemy's resistance stiffened, shells commenced to fall on fields yet unscarred by trench or shell-hole. Better ammunition seemed to be in use —or was it a month's holiday from shells that made it seem so?—and more subtlety was shown by German gunners in their choice of targets. Our casualties, though not numerous, proved that the war, in most of its old incidents, had been resumed.

In the early morning of April 4 the 59th Division, which was operating on the Battalion's left, attacked Le Vergier. Fighting continued till noon, but the village was not taken. The 59th lost heavily. As they formed up for their advance—which was for some 1,000 yards across the open and exposed to view—behind the line the Battalion was holding, considerable enemy fire was brought down upon us and I lost Sergeant Watkins, wounded in the arm, and several other casualties. It snowed nearly all day. In the shallow trenches, which were ill-sited both for drainage and concealment from the enemy, life was miserable. On the next night a battalion of Sherwood Foresters relieved D Company, which returned to its wood, but B and C Companies remained holding the line. John Stockton, who now commanded B, was ill, but refused to leave the trenches and carried on in a most determined manner under shocking weather conditions. A new officer, Allden, in my company also proved his worth about this time. Events of some sort were of hourly occurrence. The 2/5th Gloucesters held the line on the Battalion's right, near the Omignon river. One night, after a heavy bombardment with 4·2s, the Germans rushed one of their posts. It had recently been evacuated, and the enemy spent his trouble in vain.

For April 6—Good Friday, 1917—an attack on a large scale had been arranged. The 59th Division on our left, the Gloucesters and the 182nd Brigade on our right, shared in the operations. The line was to be advanced a mile on both sides of the Omignon. The Battalion's objective was a line of trenches recently dug by the enemy and running between Le Vergier and the river. To capture them Brown's company, which hitherto had stayed in reserve at Soyécourt in tolerable accommodation, was selected. B and D Companies were ordered to keep close behind A to support the attack, while C remained to garrison the outpost line.

Zero was midnight, but before that snow and sleet were falling heavily. It proved the dirtiest night imaginable. Companies moved in columns across the 1,000 yards of open fields between their old positions and the objective, against which our artillery kept up as severe a fire as possible. That fire was less effective than was hoped. In its advance A Company lost men from our own shells, of which nearly all were seen to be falling very short. The German wire, still the great argument to face in an attack, was found uncut. Although at first inclined to surrender, the enemy soon saw the failure of our men to find a gap. Machine-guns were manned, which swept the ground with a fierce enfilade fire. Brown, Aitken, and Wayte behaved in a most gallant manner, the line was rallied, and a renewed attempt made to storm the trenches. In vain. No troops will stand against machine-gun fire in the open when no object can be achieved. It was idle to repeat the attack or send fresh companies to share the forlorn enterprise. Before dawn our troops were in their old positions.

In the attack the sergeant-majors of both A and B Companies were hit. Of the officers, Barton, commanding B, and Tilly, of A, were killed. Aitken and Wayte were wounded. Nearly 40 of rank and file were casualties.

The attack had proved a failure, but, as often happened, hopes of success were reluctantly abandoned by the staff. Thus my company was warned that it might have to repeat the attack at dawn. Pending such a fate, I was sent to bivouac in a windswept spinney known as Ponne Copse. It was still snowing. After their week's exposure I was loth to inform my men of such a destiny. But a more favourable turn of events was in store. The weather cleared, and at 11 a.m. on the 7th I was allowed to return to my version of Montolu Wood. On the same day the Battalion was relieved by the Bucks and marched back through Soyécourt to Caulaincourt. There we found Bennett, who had come from the Aldershot course to be Second in Command. The château grounds were quieter than before, for our guns had now moved further up towards the line.

At 3 p.m. on April 8 a curious noise was heard in the air. A German aeroplane had attacked the kite balloon, which hung, suspended by its gas, above the château park. A French machine, not a moment too soon for the balloon's safety, had swooped and shot the attacker to the ground. All the Battalion was out staring up at the balloon rotating on its wire, and the portions of the German 'plane, which amid smoke were fluttering to earth. A rush, as always, commenced towards the scene. The aeroplane, brought down from a height, was half embedded in the mud. It was an Albatross, painted all colours, and possessed two machine-guns and several sorts of ammunition for use against balloons. I could see nothing of its former occupant, who must have been removed for burial, except a pool of bright blood upon the ground.

During the night orders arrived for a move forward to support the Warwick Brigade, which had been fighting for several days between Maissemy and Fresnoy. At 7.30 a.m. on April 9 we marched in wind and rain to Marteville, and then formed a reserve line in front of Maissemy and Keeper's House. All day we dug trenches and erected wire. A divisional relief was to take place. The weather was vile; almost every hour a violent squall of hail and snow swept over us. That night was spent in bivouac in sunken roads.

Next morning many of us walked along the Holnon road to view St. Quentin, whose cathedral and factory chimneys were only visible between the storms. The town seemed undestroyed. The Germans were busy shelling its approaches. Salvoes of their 5.9s fell steadily, and black splashes of earth jumped up ever and again, whilst smoke from the preceding shells coiled and drifted away to the west.

The 61st Division was relieved on April 11 and moved back to the Nesle area. The 2/4th Oxfords marched to Hombleux, a village where the enemy had left the church and a few houses standing.

The German retirement from the Somme, now practically complete, had opened a new phase in the war. For the first time since 1914 ground in France had changed hands upon a large scale. The enemy's relinquishment of 30 miles of front line trench and his withdrawal to a depth, in places, of 40 kilometres, restored the principle of manœuvre to armies which had fronted one another for two years in positions hitherto justifying the description of stale-mate. Strong moral and political effects accompanied. And this manœuvre, though carried out upon a part only of the entire battle front, infused a sense of change and movement into the most static portions of the allied line. From theory open warfare had passed into practice. In its old sense trench-warfare was no more; its genius had departed. Trenches and dug-outs, which in some sectors had been visited and re-visited with changeless repetition for thirty months, lost their sense of eternity. Who could say when the trenches opposite might not be found empty and the burning wake of a German retreat glow in the skies? Schemes for action in event of enemy withdrawal began to take precedence over trench standing orders. Corps lines ceased to be the show-places for Russian colonels, and the Corps Commander's gardener paused before sowing a new season's peas in the château grounds.

G.H.Q. were agog.

Chapter VIII.

THE RAID AT FAYET,

April, 1917.

A German vantage-point.—Shell-ridden Holnon.—A night of confusion.—Preparing for the raid of April 28.—The enemy taken by surprise.—The Battalion's first V.C.—The affair at Cepy Farm.

IT was hard to believe that any lofty eminence which overlooked our lines was not in constant use by the enemy for observation. The iron towers at Loos, the spire of Calonne, even the crazy relics of the church at Puisieux at different times contributed this uneasy feeling to the denizens of our trenches. But surely never was the sense of being spied on more justified than near St. Quentin, whose tall cathedral raised itself higher than all the roofs of the town and higher, too, than the ridges surrounding it for many miles.

On April 20, 1917, a German observer from the cathedral belfry could have seen the divisional relief which brought the 61st Division back to the line. All day small parties were moving in the forward zone, while further back larger ones crossed and re-crossed the ridge 'twixt Holnon and Fayet, and in rear again, along the road through Savy to Germaine, columns of Infantry in fours followed by horses, vehicles, and smoking cooker-chimneys, were passing one another, some coming, others going back. Those coming made a left-handed turn at Savy, hugged the line of single railway as far as a crucifix at a cross-roads, and were then lost to distinct view amid the abject ruins of Holnon. Those going were the 32nd Division, whose march carried them out of the cathedral's eye or observation by German balloons.

Among the new arrivals were the 2/4th Oxfords, of whom all companies, followed until the end by cookers and Lewis-gun limbers, disposed themselves in or around Fayet, on whose north side stood a stone monument commemorative of local fighting in the Franco-Prussian War. Near to this monument was found a deep sunken road, broken with two huge craters. It was A Company's position as support to the Gloucesters, who went into the line.

The Battalion spent a.week at Holnon village. A line of trenches linking up 'strong points' had been designed to guard the ridge which overlooked Fayet and St. Quentin. From Selency Château, whose thickets fringed the sky-line, on the right, to the high-perched windmill above Maissemy on the left, work to consolidate this system had commenced. It remained for us to excavate the chalk trenches deeper and erect wire. The demand for that material exceeded the supply, and it was necessary to salve old German stores. Some excellent coils I found—of American manufacture. Pickets were improvised. Thus liberated by the amateur assortment of our tools from the irksome tyranny of army wiring circulars, we set about the work and soon put up some of the best wire of my experience.

In Holnon the life was a new sample of unpleasantness. Of accommodation, save for a few low walls and half-roofed cellars, there was no trace. What Holnon lacked in billets it received in shells. With intervals—possibly only those of German mealtimes—during the day and nearly throughout the night, 5.9s and 4.2s were throwing up the brickdust, till it seemed reasonable to ask why in wonder's name the Battalion or any living soul was kept in Holnon. After a few bad nights with little sleep and some close shells, Headquarters moved from their shed, hard by a mound, to a dismantled greenhouse further back. It was a nasty time. The German aeroplanes were very active . . . .

That faint patter of machine-gun fire which comes from aeroplanes circling overhead ends in the descent of one of them. At first it seems to come down normally, yet with a sort of pilot-light twinkling at its head; but, when a hundred feet or so from earth, see it burst into a sheet of flame and shrivel up upon the ground in a column of dark smoke!

I had my company in shelters under a bank, clear of the village but immediately in front of a battery of 18-pounder guns, whose incessant firing, added to the evil whistle of the German shells, deprived the nights of comfortable sleep. But passive experiences were due to give place to active. Events of moment were in store. The 184th Brigade had been warned to carry out an 'enterprise' against the enemy. During the morning of April 26 I was sent for by the Colonel. I found Headquarters in their new position, an oblong greenhouse over whose frame, destitute of glass, was stretched a large 'trench shelter.' They had passed a shell-ridden night. Bennett just now had narrowly eluded a 5.9. This morning shells were falling as usual in Holnon, and pieces occasionally came humming down to earth close by. I listened to the plan of a large raid which with two companies I was soon to perform. Moore was here to outline the scheme and also Colonel Cotton of the R.F.A., whose guns were to support the operation.

At this point I must explain for the benefit of lay readers the difference between a raid and an attack. The purpose of the latter was to drive the enemy from ground he occupied and stay there. Early attacks upon the Western Front were usually directed against trenches, of which successive lines, reaching to a distance or 'depth' of several thousand yards, were often our goal or 'objective.' So that our Infantry could enter hostile trenches it was invariably necessary to destroy the wire in front or make a pathway through it. Many attacks failed because the wire had not been cut. Before the days of Tanks the means employed consisted, broadly speaking, in artillery fire, which it was also hoped would put the enemy's machine-guns out of action and frighten his garrison. Our Infantry advanced immediately this fire had ceased or 'lifted' to the next objective. During the Battle of the Somme it was found that the enemy often

THE RAID AT FAYET, APRIL, 1917.

left his actual trenches and came forward into shell-holes in No-Man's-Land so as to escape the fire of our artillery. To counter this manœuvre the 'creeping barrage' was devised. Our shells were fired so as to form a moving curtain of destruction immediately in front of our men in their advance, whilst at the same time the enemy's trenches were bombarded. Attacks on any scale were planned to capture and hold against the enemy some ridge, by losing which he lost observation of our lines, while we, in gaining it, saw more of his and also were enabled to advance our guns.

The purpose of a raid was to penetrate a portion of the enemy's front, to kill or capture as many Germans as possible, and then retire. Raids differed materially from attacks in this respect, that no attempt was made in the former to hold the ground won longer than was necessary to satisfy the plan. Raids were usually supported by artillery and took place at night; but daylight raids, though less common or successful, were sometimes made, and 'silent raids,' when no artillery was used, were also tried.

This explanation, dull to military readers, will serve to indicate what operation I was now about to undertake. The scheme, of which the General and his Brigade Major were the authors, was to pass a body of men through a gap in the unoccupied portion of the German trenches opposite Fayet, deploy, and sweep sideways against some other trenches, thought to be held, and through several copses which Bucks patrols had pronounced weakly garrisoned by the enemy. These copses, which were expected to yield a few handfuls of runaway boys in German uniform, would be attacked by us in flank and rear at the same time. The scheme promised well, but the proposed manner of retirement, which would be in daylight and across nearly a mile of open ground, presented difficulties. The more to overcome them and to be fresh for the event, D Company and the platoons of C selected for the task were to stay in the sunken road north of Fayet, while A and B Companies went to garrison the outpost line.

The Battalion was mostly fortunate in the opportunity of its reliefs. One always prayed that the time spent in moving up and changing places with troops in the front line would coincide with a period quiet in regard to shelling. One hoped still more that no hostile attack would clash with the relief.

Such prayers and hopes on April 26, when a quiet, easy relief was specially desired, came near to being falsified. At dusk, just as our companies were starting towards Fayet, the enemy commenced an operation against Cepy Farm, a ruined building near the front line, predestined by its position to be an object of contention. The attack was ably dealt with by Tubbs' company of the Bucks had proved abortive for the enemy. The circumstance was accompanied by much erratic shelling from both sides. Orders to stand-to were issued rather broadcast, and as the relief was now in progress a degree of confusion resulted everywhere. The destination of my company and half of C was the sunken road leading down into

THE RAID NEAR ST. QUENTIN
BY 2/4 OXFORD & BUCKS LT. INFY. AP. 28 1917

German Trenches
2nd Crater
TO ST QUENTIN 1 MILE
4 C COY
5
2
3
1 D COY
Gap
GRICOURT
184 Bde Outpost Line
1st Crater
FAYET
Chateau
R.A.P.
BATT H.Q.
The Sunken Road
THE MONUMENT
From HOLNON
Drawn by G.K. Rose

REFERENCE
☐ IIIrd JAEGERS
▨ OXFORD & BUCKS
Scale in Yards 0 — 500

1 Rose
2 Allden
3 Taylor
4 Jones
5 Butcher

Fayet, but that I found already crowded with troops. Almost all units of the Brigade seemed to be trying to relieve or support each other, and the front line itself was in quite a ferment, nobody actually knowing what the enemy had done, was doing, or was expected to do. Under these conditions it became impossible for me to send patrols to learn the ground from which the impending raid was to be launched. It happened, in fact, that when the time to move forward had arrived, I alone of all the five platoons about to be engaged knew the route to the 'position of assembly,' that is to say, the place where the attacking troops were to collect immediately before the raid. That most severe risk—for had I been a casualty the entire enterprise would have miscarried—was owing partly to the accident of the confused relief, but more to the short notice at which the work was to be carried out. Instead of that thorough reconnaissance which was so desirable I had to be content with a visit, shared by my officers and a few N.C.O.'s, to an advanced observation post from which a view was possible of those trenches and woods we were under orders to raid.

The sunken road proved anything but a pleasant waiting place. The shelling of Fayet—freshscattered bricks across whose roads showed it an unhealthy place—was now taken up in earnest by the enemy. Partly perhaps from their own affection for such places, but more probably because it was our most likely route to reach the village, the Germans seldom allowed an hour to pass without sending several salvoes of 5·9s into the sunken

THE RAID AT FAYET, APRIL, 1917.

road. My men were densely packed in holes under the banks. I was expecting large supplies of flares and bombs and all those things one carried on a raid, and had, of course, orders and explanations of their duties to give to many different parties.

All this made April 27 a vexatious day. During the early part of the night men from my company had to carry rations to the front line companies. At midnight, while resting in a wretched lean-to in the sunken road, I had tidings that Corporal Viggers and several others had been hit by a shell, which destroyed all C Company's rations. Of these casualties there was a man whose name I forget, who insisted on going, not back to hospital, but into the raid a few hours afterwards. He went, and was wounded again. It is a privilege to place on record the valorous conduct of this un-named soldier.

While I was receiving the serious news which deprived me of a valuable leader and several picked men, a shell pitched a few yards from the spot I occupied. The light went out, and I was half covered with dust and rubbish. To move was second nature. Followed by Taylor I 'moved' 100 yards down the road to the rest of my company. My kit and maps were later rescued from the dirt and brought to my new position. Company Headquarters should be mobile, and on occasions like these were volatile.

At 1 a.m. I roused the men, some 150 all told, and the responsible task of issuing the bombs, wirecutters, and other things commenced. All these, invoiced with excellent precision by the Brigade

Major, Moore, had been carried up by the Berks. The shelling rarely ceased, and I owed everything on this occasion to Corporal Leatherbarrow, who showed not only steadfast bravery but skill. The platoons could not, on account of the shells which sometimes fell in the roadway itself, be paraded, and each received its share of bombs piecemeal by sections. Food, to supplement which I did not scruple to issue some of the next day's rations, was partaken of at 2 a.m., but it took long, and half an hour later the whole party should have started upon its journey across the mile of open fields to reach the assembly post. Disposal of the bombs, the meal, and those many last attentions which breed delay had taken longer than I had allowed. Time was getting very short. I wanted to dodge the shelling, but had missed a quiet interval that occurred at 2.30 a.m. At 3 a.m. I moved, leading the party in a long column over the open ground north of Fayet to reach its eastern side. The inevitable 'wire mats,' an encumbrance without which few raiding parties ever started, hampered the progress. It was a pitch dark night, nor was I certain of the way. To cover the mile and then pass 150 men, ignorant of their whereabouts, silently and in single file through a gap into No-Man's-Land ere dawn broke and our bombardment started now seemed impossible. It was a serious quandary. To go on might be to compromise not only the operation, but the lives of 150 men, who would be discovered in daylight and in the open near the enemy. But to go back was to jeopardise the reputation of the Battalion.

THE RAID AT FAYET, APRIL, 1917.

I went on.

Great darkness preceded the dawn, which was expected shortly after 4 a.m. I found the road, the first crater, the narrow track through the wire, and the empty ground beyond. A few minutes after the last man had reached his place our barrage opened. Shells fell spasmodically here and there for a few seconds; then all our batteries were shooting together. Their fire was admirable, heavy and well-directed.

In the stumbling rush forward to reach the nearest wood—C Company to the second crater on the Fayet Road—waves and platoons were rapidly confused. The Germans, who found themselves attacked in flank and rear, were totally surprised. They had not stood-to and many were yet asleep. Some lights went up and a few sentries' shots were fired, but it appeared that small resistance to our progress would be made. The wire was trampled through, and for some minutes our men played havoc with the Germans, who ran, leaving draggled blankets and equipment in their trenches. Dug-outs were generously bombed, and explosions filled the air as our men hastily used the weapons brought to hurt the enemy. Three machine-guns fell into our hands. A miniature victory was in progress.

But a turn of events followed; the trenches and woods beyond those we had first entered were neither unoccupied nor weakly held. A force certainly equal to ours was in opposition. After their first surprise the Germans recovered, manned their reserve machine-guns, and opened a fierce fire from front and flanks upon their assailants. Many of us were hit, including Taylor, the officer of No. 15 Platoon, who was severely wounded in the thigh. In No. 13 Platoon, which lost most heavily, Allden and his Platoon Sergeant, Kilby, were killed. The full programme could not be effected. It was getting light; so I decided to withdraw. Most of D Company I found had already done this in their own way, but the remainder now collected at my summons. Lance-Corporal O'Connor with his two Lewis guns did yeoman service to stem what had become the German counter-attack. Ammunition was running short, and German stick-bombs obliged me, in order to save from capture those less badly hit, to leave Taylor, whose wound made him quite helpless. The wire, through which Sergeant Mowby had been busy cutting a path, was safely passed, and an hour afterwards we had regained the sunken road. I learnt that Jones, who had led the right of the advance, had not returned. He with his men had narrowly missed being cut off when the dawn broke. During the ensuing day this party had to lie scattered in shell-holes till darkness enabled them to reach our lines.

The raid was hailed as a signal success for the Battalion. Two machine-guns and one protesting prisoner had been dragged back to our lines. The German trenches had been over-run and many of their occupants had been killed or wounded. By a satisfactory coincidence the troops whom we surprised were a battalion of the Jaegers, the very regiment which after three hours' bombardment had raided us exactly two months previously at Ablaincourt.

COMPANY SERGEANT-MAJOR E. BROOKS, V.C.

p. 101.

THE RAID AT FAYET, APRIL, 1917.

Our losses, considering the scope of the operation, were heavy, but not so proportionately to the number of troops of both sides engaged nor to the severe nature of the fighting. Most of our casualties had bullet wounds. The list, officially, was: Killed, 1 officer and 10 other ranks; wounded, 2 officers and 41; missing, 1 officer and 2. Of Taylor I regret to say no news was ever heard. I left him wounded, probably fatally, and quite incapable of being moved. The likelihood is that he died soon afterwards and was buried by the enemy in the trench where he lay. Allden and Kilby were a serious loss to the fighting efficiency of D Company.

For their gallantry Corporal Sloper and Sergeant Butcher received the Military Medal and Jones the Military Cross. Corporal Leatherbarrow for his seadfast conduct in the sunken road was mentioned in dispatches. To Sergeant-Major Brooks fell the honour of the Battalion's first V.C., of which the official award ran as follows:—

> 'For most conspicuous bravery. This Warrant Officer, while taking part in a raid on the enemy's trenches, saw that the front wave was checked by an enemy machine-gun at close quarters. On his own initiative, and regardless of personal danger, he rushed forward from the second wave with the object of capturing the gun, killing one of the gunners with his revolver and bayoneting another. The remainder of the gun's crew then made off, leaving the gun in his possession. S.M. Brooks then turned the machine-gun on to the retreating enemy, after which he carried it back to our lines. By his courage and initiative he undoubtedly prevented many casualties, and greatly added to the success of the operations.'

Infantry's recompense for raids and attacks was usually a short rest. This time it had to be postponed by a brief tour in the front line. So the next day, having exchanged positions with a Gloucester company, we lay in holes and watched the 5.9s raising their clouds of red brick-dust in Holnon. Fayet was left alone, nor did the sunken road receive attention. It was a balmy day, the first of spring.

At night another minor operation preceded the relief. Orders were given for B Company, which held the right of the Battalion's line, to seize the much-disputed Cepy Farm and hand it over to the incoming Berks. Moberly, who had recently rejoined his old Battalion, was in command of this enterprise. The farm was reached and duly occupied, but when the time for handing over to the Berks arrived our post was driven out by a strong party of the enemy. This was the first of many similar encounters at Cepy Farm. Luckily it did not long prejudice the relief. Though chased a little on the way by shells, the Battalion had an easy march to Holnon Wood, in which a pleasant resting place was found. The trees and undergrowth, just bursting into green, presented happy contrast to the dust and danger of Fayet. In the sandy railway cutting, where the single line turns through the wood to reach Attilly, companies sat during the day and slept secure at night. Transport and cookers were near, and for a spell one was on terms of friendship with the world.

Chapter IX.

ARRAS AND AFTERWARDS,

May, June, July, 1917.

Relief by the French at St. Quentin.—A new Commanding Officer.—At the Battle of Arras.—Useful work by A Company.—Harassing fire.—A cave-dwelling.—At Bernaville and Noeux.—In G.H.Q. reserve.—A gas alarm by General Hunter Weston.—The Ypres arena.

THE next battlefield to which the Battalion's steps were turned was Arras. Early in May the French came to relieve the 61st Division at St. Quentin. It was said, perhaps with little truth, that the ban which forbade our guns to shell that town in such manner as, from a purely military standpoint, it deserved, induced this re-arrangement of the front. Certainly the French had tried in April, before the German retreat had definitely stopped, to encircle the town and capture it without bombardment, and possibly their staff yet hoped that it might fall undamaged into their hands. The attitudes of English and French artillerymen towards large towns which they saw opposite to them were naturally different. On this particular front St. Quentin was a potent hostage in the enemy's power and one which accounted for the extremely quiet conduct of the war in that sector after the English had left.

On its backward march—moves by divisions up and down the front were always made at a good distance behind the line through districts known as 'staging areas'—the Battalion spent a few days close to Amiens, and thence marched through Doullens to familiar billets at Neuvillette. The 184th Infantry Brigade reached Arras at the end of May, and went into the line on June 2.

During this move Colonel Bellamy, who had commanded us since August, 1916, left the Battalion. He shortly afterwards succeeded to the command of the 2nd Royal Sussex, his former regiment. A man of tact and ripe experience, he had done much to improve the Battalion during his stay. He lacked few, if any, of the best qualities of a Regular officer. His steady discipline, sure purpose, and soldierly outlook, had made him at once Commanding Officer, counsellor and friend. Latterly he had been somewhat vexed by illness, but had refused to allow his activity to be handicapped thereby. His stay had not coincided with the brightest nor least difficult epochs in the Battalion's history, for which reason, since he was not unduly flattered by fortune, his merit deserves recognition.

Colonel Bellamy's successor, H. de R. Wetherall, was a young man whom ability and leadership had already lifted to distinction in his regiment and placed in command of an important military school. From now onwards he is the outstanding figure in the Battalion's history. In the new Colonel a quick brain was linked with vigorous physique. In spite of his Regular training, Wetherall could appreciate and himself possessed to no small degree the peculiar virtues of the temporary officer, who based his methods on common sense and actual experience in the war rather than servile obedience to red tape and 'Regulations.' He had studied during the war as well as before it, with the result that military tradition—his regiment was the Gloucestershire—and his long service in the field combined to fit him for command of our Battalion.

The Division's share in the Arras Battle, 1917, was small. Already at the time of our arrival the later stages of the fighting had been reached. The British advance astride the River Scarpe had stopped on its north side beneath the low ridge spoken of as Greenland Hill and on its south before a wood known as the Bois du Vert. As on the Somme in November, 1916, local actions were continuing. To prepare for an attack on Infantry Hill, a position held by the enemy south-east of Monchy-le-Preux, the 2/4th Oxfords went into the front line on June 6. Orders were received to advance across No-Man's-Land and link up a line of shell-holes as a 'jumping-off place' for the subsequent attack. A Company successfully accomplished the task, and the Battalion earned a message of thanks from the Division which a few days afterwards made the designed attack.

Apart from this achievement, the confused network of old and new trenches occupied during this period offered few features of special interest. C and A Companies and part of D were in the front line, which ran through chalk and was unsavoury by reason of the dead Germans lying all about. The enemy's fire was of that harassing kind which began now to mark the conduct of the war. In the old days conventional targets such as roads, trenches, and villages within a mile or two of our front were generally shelled at times which could be guessed and when such places could be avoided. These methods changed. Wherever Infantry or transport were bound to go at special times during the night, the German shells, reserved by day, were fired. Roads, tracks, and approaches, where in daylight English nursemaids could almost have wheeled perambulators with confidence, by night became hated avenues of danger for our Infantrymen moving up the line or ration-carrying to their forward companies. The fire to which they went exposed was the enemy's 'harassing fire,' and we, in our turn, very naturally 'harassed' the Germans. At this time a crater on the Arras-Cambrai road which must needs be passed and a shallow trench leading therefrom, known as Gordon Alley, were the most evil spots. Monchy, the hill-village which had cost us so many lives to capture, was heavily shelled by German howitzers both day and night; below its slopes lay several derelict tanks. Our gun positions, in proportion to the new increase in counter-battery work, were also often shelled. Though unconnected with any artillery, our doctor, Stobie, and with him Arrowsmith had a bitter experience of German shells. One fine summer morning the enemy commenced a programme of destructive fire upon some empty gun-pits where the Doctor had his dressing-station. Stobie and

Arrowsmith, with their personnel, received a high explosive notice to quit, and their descent into a wrong-facing shaft was next followed by the partial destruction of their only exit. They escaped safely and arrived in a state of pardonable excitement at the deep cave under Les Fosses Farm, where my Company Headquarters and many others were.

This cave, perhaps, will bear a short description. In Artois and Picardy, where chalk strata prevailed, deep subterranean passages and caves abounded. Under Arras itself sufficient room existed to hold many thousands of our troops, who were housed underground before the battle opened. The Germans more than ourselves exploited this feature of geology. Under Gommecourt and Serre their reserve troops had lurked deep in caves. In the Champagne more striking instances occurred of whole battalions issuing from hidden passages and exits to the fight. The cave below Fosses Farm was about 40 feet below the ground. Of most irregular shape, it branched and twisted into numerous alleys and chambers through the chalk. In it lived representatives of the Artillery, Royal Engineers, New Zealand Tunnellers, the whole of B Company, parts of Headquarters, the Doctor's personnel, and my own Company Headquarters. The cave was dimly lit by a few candles. Throughout the day and night there were perpetual comings and goings, and it was common to see men, dazzled by the outside sun, come stumbling down the stairs and tread unseeing on the prostrate forms of those asleep below. The bare chalk was floor, bed, and bench to all alike. The shadows, the dim groups of figures, and the rough pillars forming walls and roof, gave the impression of some old cathedral. At one end a hole communicating with the ground above served as the only chimney for the incessant cooking that was going on. The fumes of this huge grill-room, which did duty, not only for the 400 men or so within the cave itself, but for as many situated at a distance in the outside world, lent a primeval stamp to the surroundings. We were cave-dwellers, living in partial darkness and lacking even the elements of furniture.

Caves, cellars, and deep dug-outs had a demoralising influence upon their occupants. The utter security below, contrasted with the danger overhead—for often the entrances to these refuges were particularly shelled—and the knowledge that at any moment the former might have to be exchanged for the latter could deal a subtle injury to one's morale. It was a golden rule, one perchance followed by many of our leaders, to make each day some expedition afield before the sun had reached its meridian. On the whole one was happier without deep dug-outs—and safer, too, for to become a skulker was equivalent to death.

In quoting things to show how little pic-nicing there was in the war I feel it opportune to mention a fresh shape in which danger now appeared, not only for the Infantry, but for others formerly immune in sheltered positions far behind the front. I refer to bombing aeroplanes. The warm clear summer nights were now, for the first time in common experience, marked by the loud droning of the enemy's machines and by the crash of bombs dropped upon huts and transport lines and along roads and railways in our back area. Arras was often severely bombed. The German aeroplanes on any fine night came to be regarded as inevitable. Bombing might be continued until nearly dawn. When no bombs fell close there was always the constant drone announcing their possibility. To men in huts or in the open, without lights or any means of shelter, the terror carried nightly overhead was greater far than that which ever served to depress Londoners.

Another development which was destined to play an ever increasing part in the war and to make its closing phases worse in some respects that its early, was the long-range high-velocity gun. Though fully seven miles behind the line, Arras was shelled throughout the summer with very heavy shells. The railway station was their principal target, but the 15-inch projectiles fell in a wide radius and caused great destruction to the houses and colleges still standing in the city. Yet to the Arras citizens now eager to return and claim their property shells seemed a small deterrent.

Our stay up in the line was short, but we had casualties. Lindsey, a new officer in D Company, was killed on his first visit to the trenches, and Herbert, of B, was wounded. D Company also lost as casualties Sergeant Buller and Lance-Corporal Barnes and half-a-dozen Lewis gunners in the line. The night of our relief was spent in bivouacs near Tilloy. A violent thunderstorm,

ARRAS—THE GRANDE PLACE.

which was the expected sequel to the fortnight's intensely warm weather we had been experiencing, drenched our surroundings and gave the hard earth, trampled by summer tracks, a surface slippery as winter mud. On June 11 the Battalion was back in billets at Bernaville, a village four miles west of Arras, and it appeared that the Division (of which the 184th Brigade alone had been into the line) had completed its tour in the Arras sector.

I rejoice that the few pleasant phases of the Battalion's experiences in France elapsed less rapidly than I describe them. At Bernaville the weather continued fine and warm; in fact, some of the hottest weather of the year occurred. A busy training programme was in swing. To escape the heat, companies paraded at 7 a.m. and worked till 11, and again in the evening at 5 and worked till 7. This training must not be judged by readers according to style and methods possibly seen by them on English training grounds during the war. At home, after the last divisions of Kitchener's Army went abroad, no officers trained their own men whom they would lead in battle. The men were usually the rawest drafts, while the officers in home battalions were too often those who had never gone and never would go to the front. A totally different spirit characterised training in France. Colonel Wetherall was a master of the art of teaching. His emphatic direction and enthusiasm earned early reward in the increased efficiency of all ranks.

At Noeux, near Auxi-le-Château, whither we moved on June 23, the Battalion's midsummer respite was continued; we were in G.H.Q. reserve. Rumour, not false on this occasion, predicted the Division's share in a great battle between Ypres and the coast which was due to happen before the autumn. Expectancy was rife to the effect that co-operation from the sea was to assist in driving the Germans from the Belgian coast. News, big in its effects, was read one morning in the *Daily Mail*. The enemy had attacked our lines at Nieuport and driven our garrison across the Yser. A valuable footing had been lost.

Happy memories are associated with Noeux. It was a pretty village, girt by rolling hills crowned with rich woods. 'Wood-fighting' (which I always said should literally mean the fighting *of* woods, and indeed it often resolved itself into a contest of man *versus* undergrowth) was a frequent feature in the training programme. What was sometimes lost in 'direction' was as often gained in naughty amusement at the miscarriage of a scheme. For off-duty hours the wild-boars of Auxi woods and the cafés in that small town provided varied attractions and romance. The General, who was delighted with the war and the Battalion, was more vigorous and inspiring than ever. It was owing largely to him that the 184th Brigade became the best in the Division. This good time, which had for its object, not enjoyment, but preparation for more fighting, came all too soon to an end.

On July 26 the Battalion said good-bye to Noeux. Its inhabitants, of whom an old lady called 'Queen Victoria' (La Reine Victoria, as she was known even by her fellow-villagers) was typi-

NOEUX VILLAGE.

cal, gave us a hearty send-off. Three hours after leaving it we again passed through the village, this time by train. We reached St. Omer in the evening and marched to a scattered Flemish hamlet called Broxeele. Here a stay longer than was expected was made; the 61st Division was in reserve to the 5th Army. The introduction by the Germans of the celebrated mustard-gas at Ypres had caused many thousand casualties in the line and lent new urgency to our gas drill.

At Broxeele on August 6 the Corps Commander, General Hunter Weston, paid a memorable visit of inspection to the Battalion. Long waits, succeeded by tedious processions of generals and decorated staff-officers of every grade, are usually associated with inspections. General Hunter Weston was more than punctual. His knowledge of all military appurtenances was encyclopedic. A rigorous examination of revolvers, mess tins, and similar accessories, at once commenced. Companies, instead of standing like so many rows of dummies, were given each some task to perform. Suddenly in the midst of everything a loud cry of 'Gas' is emitted by the General. Not unprepared for such a 'stunt' as this, the entire party scrambles as fast as possible into gas-helmets. I think we earned high marks for our gas-discipline. This inspection made a strong impression on the men, who afterwards remembered the occasion and often spoke of it.

Towards the end of July the weather, hitherto so fine, broke hopelessly. Torrential rains followed, which inundated the flat country far and wide. After several postponements the Third Battle of Ypres commenced on July 31. Some two weeks later the Battalion moved forward by train from Arnecke to Poperinghe. We awaited our share in the fighting which was to make this battle the most bloody and perhaps least profitable of the whole war.

Chapter X.

THE THIRD BATTLE OF YPRES,

August, 1917.

A Battalion landmark.—Poperinghe and Ypres.—At Goldfish Château.—The attack near St. Julien on August 22.—Its results.—A mud-locked battle.—The back-area.—Mustard gas.—Pill-box warfare.

IN the war-history of all Battalions there is a season when it is possible to say that they have reached their fulness of development, but have not yet lost all original identity. August, 1917, was such a season in my history. Of officers and men who had served with the Battalion in its infancy many were yet remaining. Time and experience of war had moulded these, with the admixture of subsequent drafts, into a Battalion sure of itself and well-developed. But when it quitted the battleground of Ypres most of its old identity had vanished. From that time onward the 2/4th Oxfords were a changed unit, whose roots were set no longer in England but in France, for in France had come to it the officers and men of whom it was afterwards constituted.

On the eve of this great change-importing battle a short review is not amiss of the Battalion's constitution. A Company still had for its Commander

Brown, among whose officers were Coombes, Callender, and Webb. As Company Sergeant Major, Cairns was a tower of strength. John Stockton led B Company, and under him was Moberly. C Company possessed two Captains, Brucker and Harris, and had as platoon commanders, Hawkes, Matthews, and Jones. D Company was still commanded by the author. An acquisition to my company had recently arrived in Scott, the bearer of two wounds received in service with the Oxford Territorials. Scott was the best officer I ever had. Guest, another new officer, before he went into the line showed that he was made of the right stuff; he was commander of No. 16 Platoon. Dawson-Smith, Copinger, Gascoyne, and Hill were other new arrivals in my company. The N.C.O.'s on whom I most relied were Sergeants Palmer, Leatherbarrow, and Sloper, but the real backbone of the Company were the gallant and determined section leaders whom I had chosen for promotion from the ranks. Of my runners and signallers I was especially proud, and at Company Headquarters there was, of course, the redoubtable Sergeant-Major Brooks, who besides being a great fighter possessed also high organising powers. My total strength on reaching Poperinghe was over 200, which shows that at this time the Battalion was well found in men. It was known nevertheless that some reduction from this maximum fighting force was to take place. One hundred men of the Battalion, including 'specialists' like Lewis gunners, signallers and runners, were henceforward 'left out of the line' whenever the Battalion went

POPERINGHE FROM THE WEST.

forward to take part in an attack. They were so left in order that, if the casualties were very high, some nucleus of veteran soldiers would still remain around whom the new Battalion could be built. A like rule applied to officers. A month ago the Colonel had decided which of these should not take part in the first Ypres attack. Brown and myself stayed out of the line, and in our stead Callender and Scott respectively commanded A and D Companies.

Our stay near Poperinghe was short. Attention was devoted to the final organisation of platoons and sections and to the problem of what kit to carry in the attack and how best to carry it. Varied experiments were made to see whether a pack or haversack was better and which way uppermost a shovel should be slung. Supply of ammunition for the Lewis guns raised many questions for debate. When all the sections—the Lewis-gunners, bombers, rifle-grenadiers, and riflemen—were finally complete, a new drain was made on our numbers by the demand for seventeen men per Company, who from their duties became known as 'Loaders and Leaders.' Their function was to lead forward during battle mules loaded with rations, water, and ammunition. So little advancing was there that the mules, so far as this Battalion was concerned, were never used, and the loaders and leaders, thanks to their function proving illusory, escaped all share in the fighting.

If Poperinghe and Ypres had quite borne out their reputations I should not here remark on either of them. The former was a most crowded and degenerate-looking town, by a few towers rendered impressive from a distance, but in reality of mean structure. Besides its club—at which I recollect that Heidsieck 1906 was then only ten francs the bottle—and its estaminets, the town held few attractions. Damage by long-range German guns around the station had been considerable, but to the town itself, except its windows, not very much had up till now occurred. The surrounding country was neither flat nor uninteresting. The Mont des Cats and Kemmel bounded the horizon on the southeast, while to the west and north gently undulating hills, covered with fields of hops, distinguished this area from the sodden plains commonly credited to Flanders. Ypres, though destroyed past any hopes of restoration, in 1917 still wore the semblance of a town. From previous descriptions of the 'Salient' I had almost expected that a few handfuls of ashes would be of Ypres the only vestige left. The portions least destroyed in Ypres compared perhaps equally with the worst in Arras, but of the two the Flemish city had been the less well-built. The remains of the great Cloth Hall, cathedral, and other buildings revealed that what had once been, supposedly, of stone was in reality white brick.

On August 18, starting at 4 a.m., the Battalion marched to Goldfish Château, close to Ypres, and the Transport to a disused brickfield west of Vlamertinghe. We lived in bivouacs and tents and were much vexed by German aeroplanes, and to a less degree by German shells. On August 20, while companies were making ready for the line,

THE THIRD BATTLE OF YPRES, AUGUST, 1917.

an air fight happened just above our camp. Its sequel was alarming. A German aeroplane fell worsted in the fight, and dived to ground, a roaring mass of fire, not forty yards from our nearest tents. By a freak of chance the machine fell in a hole made by a German shell. The usual rush was made towards the scene—by those, that is, not already sufficiently close for their curiosity. A crowd, which to some extent disorganised our preparations for the line, collected round the spot and watched the R.F.C. extract the pilot and parts of the machine, which was deeply embedded in the hole. For hours the wreckage remained the centre of attraction to many visitors. The General hailed the burnt relics, not inappropriately, as a lucky omen.

During the night of August 20/21 the Battalion relieved a portion of the front eastward of Wieltje. Three companies were placed in trenches bearing the name of 'Capricorn,' but B was further back. During the night a serious misfortune befell the latter. Three 5.9s fell actually in the trench and caused thirty-five casualties, including all the sergeants of the company. On the eve of an attack such an occurrence was calculated to affect the morale of any troops. That the company afterwards did well was specially creditable in view of this demoralising prelude.

On the following night Companies assembled for the attack. Neither the starting place nor the objectives for this are easily described by reference to surrounding villages. The nearest was St. Julien. The operation orders for the attack of

August 22 assigned as objective to the Oxfords a road running across the Hanebeck and referred to as the Winnipeg-Kansas Cross Road. The 48th Division on the left and the 15th on the right were to co-operate with the 184th Brigade in the attack.

Shortly before 5 the bombardment started. In the advance behind the creeping barrage put down by our guns, of which an enormous concentration was present on the front, C, D and A Companies (from right to left) provided the first waves, while B Company followed to support the flanks. The Berks came afterwards as 'moppers up.' Half-an-hour after the advance started D, B and A Companies were digging-in 150 yards west of the Winnipeg-Kansas Cross Road. The losses of these companies in going over had not been heavy, but, as so often happens, casualties occurred directly the objective had been duly reached. In the case of C Company, on the right, but little progress had been made. Pond Farm, a concrete stronghold, to capture which a few nights previously an unsuccessful sally had been made, had proved too serious an obstacle. Not till the following night was it reduced, and during the whole of August 22 it remained a troublesome feature in the situation. Before the line reached could be consolidated or they could act to defeat the enemy's tactics, our men found themselves the victims of sniping and machine-gun fire from Schuler Farm, which was not taken and to which parties of reinforcements to the enemy now came. More dangerous still was an old gun-pit which lay behind the left flank. The capture of this had been assigned to the 48th Divi-

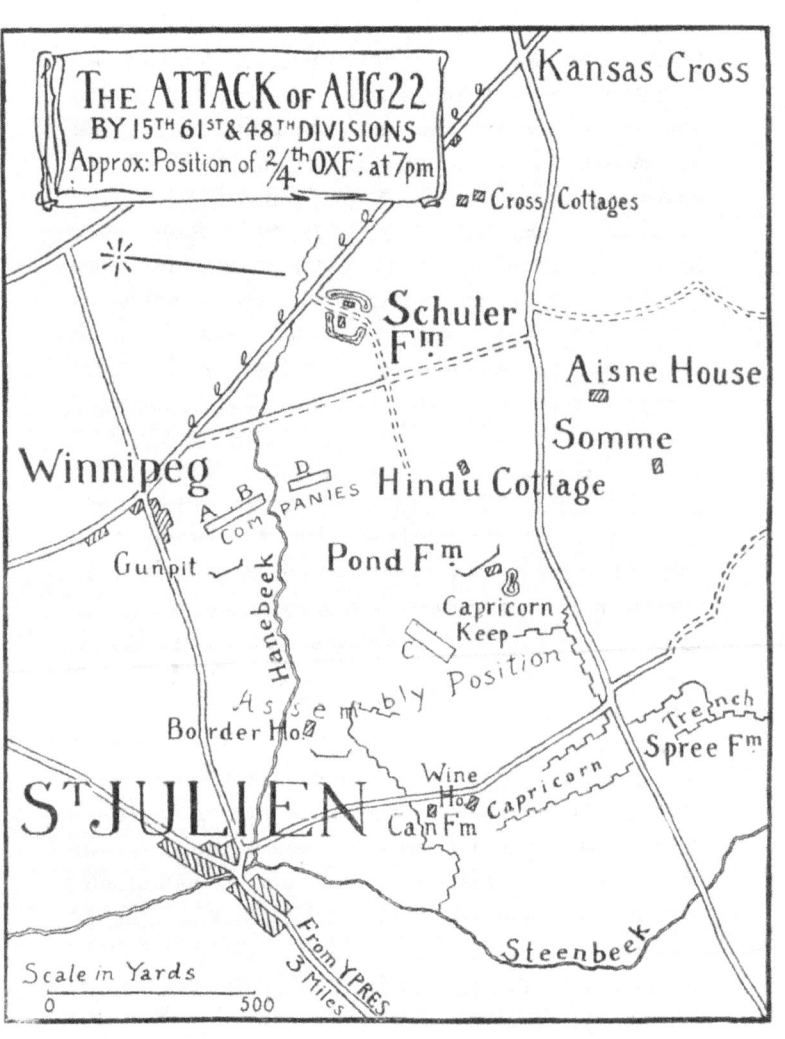

sion, but as a measure of abundant caution Colonel Wetherall had detailed a special Berks platoon to tackle it. This platoon, assisted by some Oxfords on the scene, captured the gun-pit and nearly seventy prisoners, but failed to garrison it. A party of the enemy found their way back and were soon firing into our men from behind.

During the early stages of consolidation, when personal example and direction were required, John Stockton, Scott, and Gascoyne were all killed by snipers or machine-gun fire. Scott had been hit already in the advance and behaved finely in refusing aid until he had despatched a message to Headquarters. While he was doing so three or four bullets struck him simultaneously and he died.

Throughout the 22nd no actual counter-attack nor organised bombardment by the enemy took place, but much sniping and machine-gun fire continued, making it almost impossible to move about. Our loss in Lewis-gunners was particularly heavy. Callender, the acting company commander of A Company, had been killed before the attack commenced, and Sergeant-Major Cairns was now the mainstay of that company, whose men were thoroughly mixed up with B. Upon the left the 48th Division had failed to reach Winnipeg, with the result that this flank of A and B Companies was quite in the air. On the Battalion's right the failure of C Company, in which Brucker had been wounded, to pass Pond Farm left the flank of D Company exposed and unsupported. But the position won was kept. Ground to which the advance had been carried with cost would not be lightly given up. Moberly, Company Sergeant-Major Cairns, and Guest—the latter by volunteering in daylight to run the gauntlet of the German snipers back to Headquarters—greatly distinguished themselves in the task of maintaining this exposed position during the night of August 22 and throughout August 23. Some of our men had to remain in shell-holes unsupported and shot at from several directions for over fifty hours. During the night of August 23/24 the Battalion was relieved, when those whom death in battle had not claimed nor wounds despatched to hospital marched back through Ypres to the old camp at Goldfish Château.

The attack, in which the Bucks had successfully co-operated on the right of our advance, earned credit for the Brigade and the Battalion. It had been, from a fighting standpoint, a military success. But from the strategical aspect the operations showed by their conclusion that the error had been made of nibbling with weak forces at objectives which could only have been captured and secured by strong. Moreover, the result suggested that the objectives had been made on this occasion for the attack rather than the attack for the objectives. The 184th Brigade had played the part assigned to it completely and with credit, but what had been gained by it with heavy loss was in fact given up by its successors almost at once. Withdrawal from the Kansas trenches became an obvious corollary to the German omission to counter-attack against them. Ground not in dispute 'twas not worth casualties to hold. On the Battalion's front Pond

Farm, a small concrete stronghold, remained the sole fruit of the attack of August 22. It was after the 61st Division had been withdrawn, wasted in stationary war, that what success could be associated with this third battle of Ypres commenced. Judged by its efforts, the 61st was ill paid in results.

On August 25 the Battalion, and with it the rest of the Brigade, moved back from Goldfish Château to Query Camp, near Brandhoek. The weather, which had been fairly fine for several weeks, now again broke in thunderstorms and rain. Trees were blown down along the main road to Ypres. The clouds hung low or raced before the wind, so that no aeroplane nor kite-balloon could mount the sky. This meteorological revulsion stood the Germans in great stead. Mud and delay, fatal to us, were to them tactical assets of the highest value. As can easily be appreciated, to postpone a complicated attack is a proceeding only less lengthy and difficult than its preparation, nor can attacks even be cancelled except at quite considerable notice. Thus it befell that some of our attacks, before they had commenced, were ruined by deluges of rain when it was too late to change the plans. On August 27 a further attack upon Gallipoli, Schuler Farm and Winnipeg was made by the 183rd Brigade in co-operation with the 15th and 48th Divisions. The mud and enemy machine-gun fire alike proved terrible. The contact aeroplane soon crashed, the advance failed to reach the 'pill-boxes' from which the Germans held out, and before night a return had to be made to the original line.

On August 30 the Brigade went forward once again to Goldfish Château. The camp had not been improved by our predecessors, who had attempted to dig in. Holes filled with water were the result, and nearly all the tents and shelters had to be moved. Since the stagnation of the battle German shelling in the back area had much increased. The field where the camp lay was bounded on three sides by railways or roads. Some of our 12-inch howitzers were close in front. Despite our best attempts to sever association with such targets we had a share in the shells intended for them. One night especially the long howl of German shells ended in their arrival very near our tents. The latter had been placed at one side of the field in order to escape, as we expected, the shells more likely to be aimed by German gunners at the main road and railway as targets. We changed our 'pitch,' but the next morning came a pursuing shell on an old line of fire, which made it clear that the best place was the deliberate middle of the field.

The passage overhead of German aeroplanes made nights uneasy. Darkness was lit by those huge flashes in the sky, which denoted explosions of our dumps of shells. The ground shook many times an hour with great concussions. Sometimes the crash of bombs and patter of machine-guns firing at our transport lasted till pale dawn appeared or its approach was heralded by the bombardment of our guns, whose voice pronounced the prologue of attack.

On both sides the concentration of artillery was

very great. Though the bad weather had shackled our advance from the start, our staff yet hoped to gain the ridge of Passchendaele before winter set in. The Germans, too, held that the stake was high. Our guns, which were advanced as far as Wieltje and St. Jean and stood exposed in the open, became the object of persistent German shelling. Sound-ranging and aerial photography had reached a high development, and few of our batteries went undiscovered. For the Artillery life became as hard as for the Infantry. Gunner casualties were very numerous. Our batteries for hours on end were drenched in mustard-gas. Into Ypres as well large quantities of 'Yellow Cross' shells, cleverly mixed up with high-explosive, were fired with nocturnal frequency. The long range of the enemy's field-guns made the effect of these subtle gas-shells, whose flight and explosion were almost noiseless amid the din of our own artillery, especially widespread. The enemy's activity against our back area was at its height at the end of August, 1917. Casualty Clearing Stations were both bombed and shelled. Near Poperinghe nurses were killed. No service forward of Corps Headquarters but had its casualties. Our lorry-drivers' work was fraught with danger. The Germans were waging a war to the knife and employing every means to serve their obstinate resistance.

The 'defence in depth,' practised to some extent at Arras, had become the enemy's reply to our destruction by artillery of the trench systems on which, earlier in the war, he had relied with confidence. Destruction of prepared positions had

VLAMERTINGE—THE ROAD TO YPRES.

reached so absolute a stage that the old arguments of wire and machine-guns brought up from deep dug-outs to fire over parapets, were no longer present. The ground to a distance of several thousand yards behind the enemy's front line could be, and had been, churned and rechurned into one brown expanse. For four miles east of Ypres there was no green space and hardly a yard of ground without its shell-hole. Positions where the enemy held out consisted in groups of concrete 'pill-boxes,' which had been made from Belgian gravel and cement in partial anticipation of this result of the artillery war. They in all cases were carefully sited and so small (being designed to hold machine-guns and their teams) that their destruction by our heavy shells was almost impossible. These 'pill-boxes' were also so designed as to support each other, that is to say, if one of them were captured, the fire of others on its flanks often compelled the captors to yield it up. Garrisons were provided from the *élite* of the German army. One cannot but admire the steadfastness with which, during this phase of warfare, these solitary strongholds held out. Indeed, the only way to cope with this defence was to press an advance on a wide front to such a depth as to reduce the entire area in which these pill-boxes lay into our possession. By attacking spasmodically we played the enemy's game.

Our methods of attack which had been practised through the spring and summer still consisted, broadly speaking, in the advance of lines of Infantry behind a creeping barrage. These lines were too often held up by pill-boxes, against which the creeping barrage was ineffectual, and once delay which had not been calculated on occurred, the creeping barrage was proved doubly useless, for it had outdistanced the speed of the advance. The change in tactics necessary to reduce these concrete strongholds was soon appreciated, but troops who had been trained in the older methods were slow, in action, to adopt the new ones requisite. Partly from such a reason the 61st Division scored little success against the pill-box defence, but lack of tangible results was not joined with lack of honest attempts. The mud, the nibbling tactics passed down from above, inadequate co-operation by the divisions fighting side by side with us, and the failure of our artillery to hit the pill-boxes which we had hoped could be put out of action by our heavy shells, further combined to paralyse efforts which, had they been directed to more easy tasks, would now, as often, have earned for the Division the highest military success.

Chapter XI.

THE ATTACK ON HILL 35,

September, 1917.

Iberian, Hill 35, and Gallipoli.—The Battalion ordered to make the seventh attempt against Hill 35.—The task.—A and D Companies selected.—The assembly position.—Gassed by our own side.—Waiting for zero.—The attack.—Considerations governing its failure.—The Battalion quits the Ypres battlefield.

'AT 4 p.m.' said the 61st Divisional Summary for the twenty-four hours ending 12 noon, September 11, 1917, 'we attacked the Battery Position on Hill 35. This attack was not successful.' A grim epitaph. The terse formula, as though wasted words must not follow wasted lives, was the official record of the seventh attempt to storm Hill 35.

Against the concrete gunpits which crowned this insignificant ridge the waves of our advance on July 31 had lapped in vain. Minor attacks designed to take Gallipoli, a German stronghold set behind the ridge, and against the sister position of Iberian on its flank, proved throughout August some of the most costly failures in the 5th Army operations. The defence of the three strongholds, Iberian, Hill 35, and Gallipoli provided a striking example of German stubbornness and skill, but added an object-lesson in the squandering of our efforts in attack. Operations upon a general scale having failed to capture all three, it was fantastically hoped that each could be reduced separately. Iberian, Hill 35, and Gallipoli supported one another, nor was it feasible to hold any without holding all. Yet to take Hill 35 on September 9 the 2/4th Oxfords were specially selected. The spirit of A and D Companies, chosen by Colonel Wetherall for the attack, was excellent. We confidently believed that we could succeed where others failed. Optimism, so vital an ingredient in morale, was a powerful assistant to the English Army. It was fostered, perhaps unconsciously, throughout the war by the cheerful attitude preserved by our Generals and staff, but its foundation lay in our great system of supply. The A.S.C., which helped to win our victories, helped, too, to temper our defeats.

On September 7 Brown and myself went up through Ypres to view the scene of the attack. At Wieltje, where Colonel Wetherall and B and C Companies already were, we descended to a deep, wet dug-out and that night listened to a narrative brought by an officer who had participated in the last attempt to take the hill. He dispensed the most depressing information about the gunpits, the machine-guns, the barrages, and last, but not least terrible (if believed), the new incendiary Verey lights used by the Germans to cremate their assailants. The description of a piece of trench, which we were to capture and block, particularly flattered

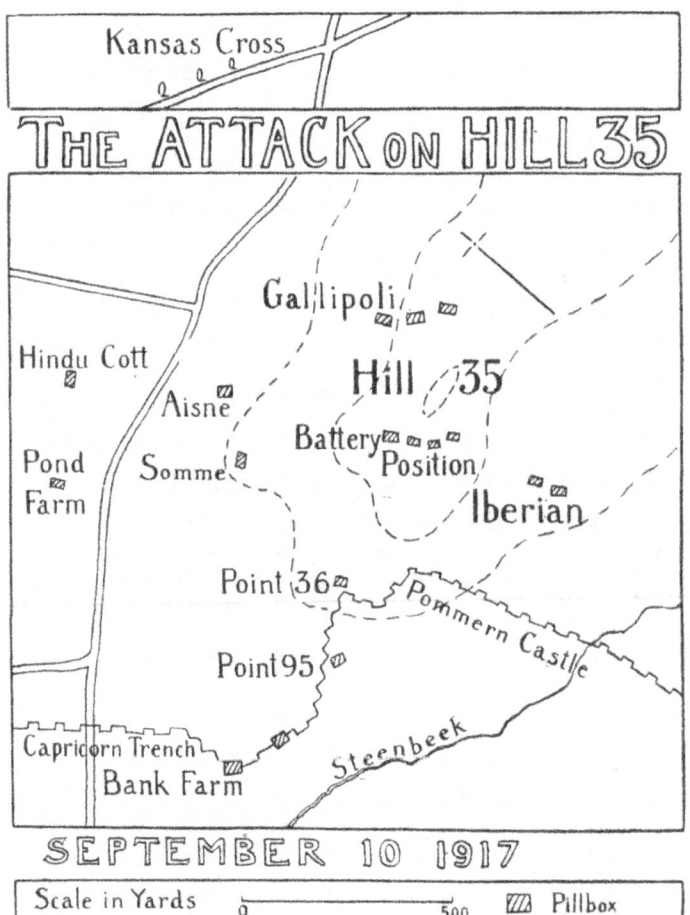

our prospects. 'Wide, shallow trench, enfiladed from Gallipoli, filled with —th Division dead,' it ran. The tale of horror becoming ludicrous, we soon afterwards clambered on to the wire bunks and slept, dripped on, till the early morning.

The next day was misty. Our 15-inch howitzers, on whose ability to smash the enemy's concrete strongholds reliance was staked, could not fire. The attack was postponed until September 10, but that decision came too late to stop our companies quitting the camp according to previous orders and marching up through Ypres. They could have stayed at Wieltje for the night, but the men's fear that by so doing they would miss their hot tea, decided their vote in favour of a return to Goldfish Château. Tea is among the greatest bribes that can be offered to the British soldier.

Accordingly the march through Ypres, or rather, round it (for no troops chose to pass its market place) was repeated on the morrow. The tracks towards the line were shelled on our way up, but we came safely through. Dusk was awaited in a much war-worn trench in front of Wieltje.

As daylight fades we file away, each man with his own thoughts. Whose turn is it to be this journey?

Along the tortuous track of tipsy duckboards we go for a mile, until acrid fumes tell that the German barrage-line is being passed. This is a moment to press on! To get the Company safely across this hundred yards is worth many a fall.

. . . Presently the shattered pollards of the

Steenbeek are left behind and flickering Verey lights cast into weird relief the rugged surface of the earth. At Pommern Castle our front trenches, in which figures of men loom indistinctly, are reached. At one corner, where the trench is littered with fragments, we are cautioned by a sentry, whose voice is a little shaken, not to linger; the entrance to a pill-box (which faced the enemy) was hit a short time ago. From the trench we proceed further into No-Man's-Land, where the Bucks are said to have linked up shell-holes since night-fall. (Those will be our 'assembly position' for the attack to-morrow afternoon).

By now all shells are passing over our heads; we are level with where Verey lights are falling, and the sweep of bullets through the air shows that the enemy is not far off. Figures appear as if by magic. All at once there is a crowd of men, rattling equipment and talking in suppressed voices. A few commands, and the relief is complete. We are in No-Man's-Land, strung in a line of shell-holes, from which in sixteen hours' time the attack is to start.

*   *   *   *

Soon after 3 a.m. I set out to visit all the scattered groups of men to give my last instructions, for from dawn onwards no movement would be possible. It was an eerie situation. The night was filled with multifarious noise—peculiar 'poops,' the distant crash of bombs, and all the mingled echoes of a battlefield. At one time German howitzers, firing at longest range, chimed a faint chorus high above our heads; anon a hissing swoop would plant a shell close to our whereabouts. Lights rose and sank, flickering. Red and green rockets, as if to ornament the tragedy of war, were dancing in the sky. Occasionally a gust of foul wind, striking the face, could make one fancy that Death's Spectre marched abroad, claiming her children. . . . .

Our guns fired incessantly. Their shells came plunging down with an arriving whistle that made each one as it came seem that it must drop short —and many did. Mist drifted fitfully around and hid, now and again, two derelict tanks, at which a forward post of my company was stationed. This post I was on my way to visit, when, suddenly, what seemed trench-mortar bombs began to fall. About twenty fell in a minute, the last ones very close to where I stood.

They were gas. It was a sickening moment; surprise, disaster, and the possibility that here was some new German devilry fired at us from behind, joined with the fumes to numb the mind and powers. Half-gassed I gave the gas-alarm. By telephone I managed to report what had happened. The Colonel seemed to understand at once; 'I've stopped them,' conveyed everything of which it was immediately necessary to make certain.

For it was an attack by our own gas. Some detachment, without notifying our Brigade staff or selecting a target which sanity could have recommended, had done a 'shoot' against my company's position under the mistake that the enemy was in

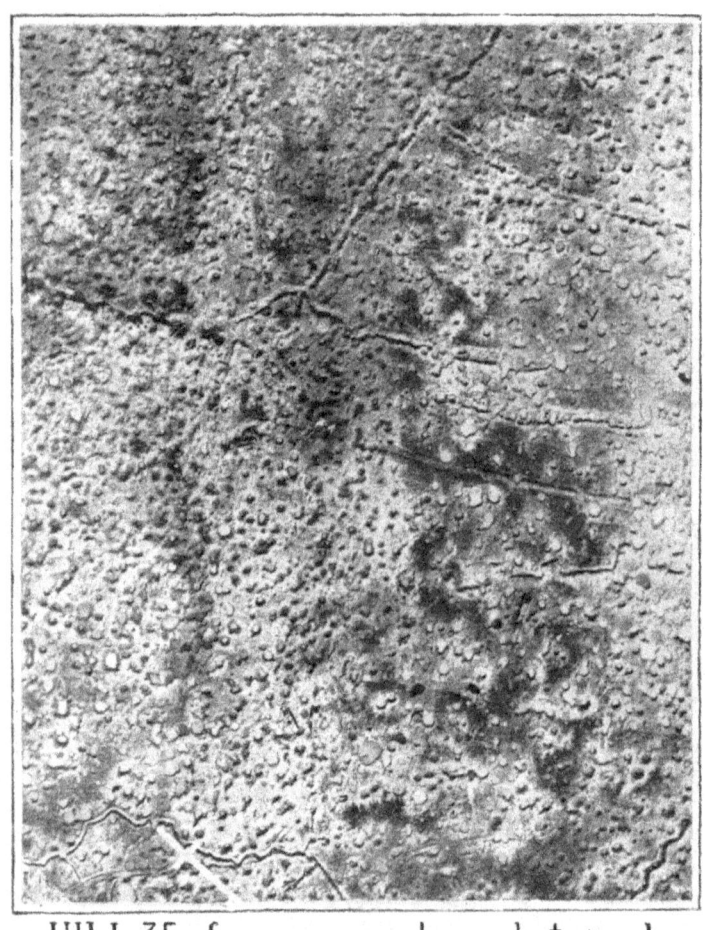

HILL 35, from an aeroplane photograph taken a week before the attack of Sept 10.

Note the four derelict Tanks

it. Two casualties, which I believe proved fatal, resulted. Many men vomited. I was prostrated for two hours. The effect on the morale of some of my men was as pitiable as it was amply justifiable.

For this dastardly outrage I fancy that no person was ever brought to book. Infantry loyally condoned the so-called 'short shooting' by our guns. Out of thousands of shells fired at the enemy some must and did fall in our lines. But from such condonation is specifically to be excepted this instance of a gas projection carried out with criminal negligence upon my comrades. For or by its perpetrator no excuse was offered; and yet the facts were never in dispute.

Proverbially the worst part of an attack was waiting for it. On September 10, from dawn till 4 p.m., A and D Companies lay cramped in shell-holes on the slopes of Hill 35. In my own hole, so close that our knees touched, sat Sergeant Palmer, Rowbotham, my signalling lance-corporal, Baxter, another signaller, Davies, my runner, and myself. With us we had a telephone and a basket of carrier pigeons.

At 8 a.m., while some of us were sleeping heavily, there came a crash and a jar, which shook every fibre in the body. An English shell had burst a yard or two from the hole wherein we lay. Voices from neighbouring shell-holes hailed us—'Are you all right?': and we replied 'We are.' We had no other shell as close as that, but all day long there were two English guns whose shells, aimed at the Germans on the ridge in front, fell so near to where we lay that we became half-used to being spattered with their earth. As the air warmed the error of these guns decreased, but we counted the hours anxiously until the attack should liberate us from such cruel jeopardy.[1]

The intolerable duration of that day baffles description. The sun, which had displaced a morning mist, struck down with unrelenting rays till shrapnel helmets grew hot as oven-doors. Bluebottles (for had not six attempts failed to take the hill?) buzzed busily. The heat, our salt rations, the mud below, the brazen sky above, and the suspense of waiting for the particular minute of attack, vied for supremacy in the emotions. The drone of howitzers continued all the day. Only at 2.30 p.m., when a demonstration was made against Iberian, did any variety even occur. There was no choice nor respite. Not by one minute could the attack be either anticipated or postponed.

Of the attack itself the short outline is soon given. Promptly at 4 p.m. the creeping barrage started. In a dazed way or lighting cigarettes the men, who had lost during the long wait all sense of their whereabouts, began to stumble forward up the hill. Our shrapnel barrage was not good. One

---

[1] At this stage in the war the barrels of many of our guns and howitzers in use on the Western Front were very worn. That fact alone and not any want of care or devotion on the part of our Artillery or staff would have accounted for the 'short shooting' which I record. To locate a worn barrel, when scores of batteries were bombarding together according to a complicated programme, was naturally impossible. Infantry recognised this.

of the earliest shells burst just behind the hole from which I stepped. It wounded Rowbotham and Baxter (my two signallers) and destroyed the basket of carrier pigeons. Of other English shells I saw the brown splash amongst our men. Prolonged bombardment had ploughed the ground into a welter of crumbling earth and mud. Our progress at only a few dozen yards a minute gave the Germans in their pill-boxes ample time to get their machine-guns going, while correspondingly the barrage passed away from our advance in its successive lifts. Heavy firing from Iberian commenced to enfilade our ranks. Long before the objective was approached our enemies, who in some cases left the pill-boxes and manned positions outside, were masters of the situation. The seventh attempt had failed to struggle up the slopes of Hill 35.

Despite the disappointment of this immediate failure of the enterprise, I realised at once the impossibility of its success. Yet on this occasion less was done by the men than the conduct of their leaders deserved. Almost as soon as bullets had begun to bang through the air some men had gone to shelter. Those who stood still were mown down. A handful of D Company, led by the company commander, by short rushes reached a ruined tank, close to the enemy, but the remainder disappeared into shell-holes, whence encouragement was powerless to move them. Only in A Company was any fire opened.

No sense of anti-climax could be demanded of the English soldier, whose daily shilling was paid him whether he was in rest-billets, on working-party, or sent into the attack.[1]

On the part also of the Artillery less was done than the scheme promised or our attacking Infantry had counted on. By shell-fire the issue of Hill 35 was to have been placed beyond doubt. When the artillery machine broke down, achievement of success demanded more initiative on the part of the Infantry than if no artillery had been used. In a sense our loss of a hundred guns at Cambrai a few weeks later became a blessing in disguise, for it restored the scales in favour of the Infantryman as the decisive agent on the field of battle.

So ended the attack on Hill 35. Upon its slopes were added our dead to the dead of many regiments. But our casualties were few considering that the attack had been brought to a standstill by machine-gun fire. Of D Company officers Guest was wounded (he had behaved with gallantry in the attack) and Copinger missing. Viggers, a very brave sergeant, was killed. Three lance-corporals, Wise, Rowbotham, and Goodman, had been wounded. The total casualties to the Battalion, including several in B Company Headquarters from a single shell and others in passing afterwards through Ypres, were, happily, under fifty.

A few days after its attack on Hill 35 the Battalion marched away from Ypres, never to

---

[1] Nowhere is this truth better expressed than in the words of 'Tommy's' own song, the refrain of which ends:—
 'But you get your "bob" a day, never mind!'

return. What credit had been earned there by the 61st Division was principally associated with the work of the 184th Infantry Brigade and of the 2/4th Oxfords. Improvement in morale flowed from the test of this great battle. The losses of the Battalion had been heavy; fourteen officers and 260 men were its casualties. The final winning of the war could not be unconnected with such a sacrifice. Like others before and others after it, the Battalion at Ypres gave its pledge to posterity.

Chapter XII.

AUTUMN AT ARRAS AND THE MOVE TO CAMBRAI,

October, November, December, 1917.

The Battalion's return to Arras.—A quiet front.—The Brigadier and hi staff.—A novelty in tactics.—B Company's raid.—A sudden move.—The Cambrai front.—Havrincourt Wood.—Christmas at Suzanne.

FROM Arras the 61st Division came to Ypres; to Arras it returned. After a week spent in the back area, advance by the usual stepping stones was made to the front line. The 184th was the last Brigade to go into the trenches; not till the beginning of October did it take over the line. The front held by the 61st Division stretched from the Chemical Works of Roeux upon the right to a point south of Gavrelle upon the left. Two Brigades were in the line at once and stayed twenty-four days, Battalions changing places during the period. A rest of twelve days back at Arras followed.

This process of relief and the general conditions brought a return of trench-warfare almost on its old lines. As autumn waned gumboots were even spoken of. The trenches were mostly of chalk, and had been left by the 17th Division in excellent condition. The experience of a former winter prevented the error being made, at all events in theory, of leaving trenches unfloored and unrevetted, until winter, bringing its consequence of mud, arrived. Especially the mile-long communication trenches called 'Chili' and 'Civil' Avenues, if they were to be kept passable, required attention. A thorough programme of work with R.E. and the Pioneers was put in hand. Dry trenches would have repaid its labour spent in carrying and digging, had the Battalion stayed in this sector for the winter. As not unexpectedly happened, we had left the scene of our labours before winter set in.

More than three weeks of October were spent by the Battalion in the trenches. This was no great hardship. Half of the time was spent nearly two miles behind the line in an old German trench known as the Gavrelle Switch. In this position there was little restriction, if indeed there could ever be any—short of its prohibition—on the making of smoke, and with good rations and day working parties the men were happy enough. But these long periods in the trenches, when no proper parades or drill were possible, though acquiesced in by the men themselves, were bad for the Battalion's discipline. Much regard was always paid —especially in the 61st Division—to what is called 'turn out.' This meant more than button-polishing. It was that quality of alertness and self-respect which even in the trenches could be maintained. Trench-life bred loafers, and loafers never made the best soldiers. It was a good thing when October 28 came and the Battalion moved back to Arras for a twelve days' spell in rest. Billets were the French prison, whose cells provided excellent accommodation.

Arras in the autumn of 1917 was an attractive place. The clear atmosphere, through which the sun shone undimmed by factory-smoke, lent to its majestic ruins almost Italian colouring. Upon the western side of the town quite a number of undamaged houses still remained; at its centre the theatre and concert hall had luckily escaped destruction, and to hear the various divisional troupes most crowded audiences assembled every night. The streets, though unlighted, were thronged with jostling multitudes. The Arras front, as though in acknowledgement of greater happenings elsewhere, had become dormant since midsummer. Against the trenches themselves little activity by the enemy was shown, and in the back area, pending a change of policy by us, quietude reigned during the early autumn. A big German gun occasionally threw its shells towards our Transport lines at St. Nicholas or into Arras Station. One day a party which had come several hours early to secure good places on the leave train was scattered by the unscheduled arrival of a shell.

During the stay of the Battalion at the prison, Thomas, our champion boxer, issued a challenge to the divisions near the town. A man from the 15th Division, heavier than Thomas, accepted. In the fight which ensued before many spectators the

A STREET IN ARRAS.

Oxford man won on a knock-out in the fourth round. So strong at this time was the Battalion in boxing that Brigade competitions became foregone conclusions.

Another feature of this period was a Brigade school, with Bennett as its commandant, at Arras. A week's course was held for each platoon in the Brigade. The school was well run and partly recompensed for the lack of training during the long tours in the trenches.

More than a year had passed since General White first took command of the 184th Infantry Brigade. During that time the Brigade had improved out of all recognition. For such result its commander was more than partially responsible. The General had to the full the quality called 'drive'; that, rather than profound knowledge of military science, made him a first-rate Brigadier. War is a department of the world's business, in which capacity not only to work oneself, but to make others work, begets success. I should hesitate to say of General White that he 'used' others, but his prudent selection of subordinates ensured that all units in his Brigade were well commanded. He was more than a good judge of character; hollow prevarication was useless with him, and bluff—though, when he liked, he was himself a master of it—a dangerous policy. Among the shrewd qualities of this man there were the abilities to summarize rapidly whatever he had been told, and to remember most of everything he saw. His power of observation was so developed that sometimes the actual picture of some detail—such as a dirty rifle, a man without equipment, or a few sand bags laid awry—lent him a false impression of the whole. Yet his memory and rapid power of observation made him a real tactician—I use the adjective advisedly. No man who knew less, and there were few who knew more, of the front line than he did, could afford to argue with him about the position of a machine-gun, although if the matter had been presented as of theory at some headquarters rather than upon the ground, the machine-gun expert would perhaps have held his own.

'Bobbie' did not interfere with his staff officers in their 'paper-work,' but if ever occasion demanded he did not hesitate to draw his pen, not in self-defence, but in defence of the Brigade and his subordinates. He was no party to that unctuous politeness that sprang up during the war when staff met staff upon the telephone. He thought nothing of ringing up Corps, and expected speech with the head of a department, for he was the enemy of all high-placed obstructionists. His fame spread widely on the telephone. Impatient of camouflage, he learnt with difficulty the language of code-names under which it was sought to disguise our units to the enemy. 'Brigadier of 184 speaking,' he would say; 'Are you the Bucks . . . What regiment are you?' There was an 'amplifier' at 'Tank Dump'; it was always most faithfully manned about 8 p.m.

The example which the General set was especially fine. He spent every day and nearly all day in the front line. Nothing annoyed him more than, say, at 9 a.m. to receive the message of a divisional conference fixed for his headquarters at 11.

"TANK DUMP"

Equipped in his short overalls and shrapnel-helmet (conspicuous in a light cover) and carrying a white walking-stick, he used to quit Brigade Headquarters with matutinal punctuality. His outset borrowed something of the atmosphere of 'John Peel' on a fine morning. Battalion Headquarters, if not warned surreptitiously of his arrival, would scramble through their breakfast (not that the General designed to interfere either with rest or eating) as his form outlined itself in the doorway, accompanied by cheery greeting. In the front line itself his visits were refreshing. Prospects of shelling never deterred him. No post was too far forward for him to pay it a call. Often, when shells fell, he deliberately remained to share the danger. Once I knew him to return to a trench, which had been quite heavily shelled while he was there, because the Germans started on it again. A prodigious walker, he tired of daylight imprisonment to trenches and chose the 'top.' His figure must have been familiar to enemy observers. But his route was so erratic that, though he drew fire on many unexpected places after he had left, he was rarely himself shot at during his progress.

The General is a great representative of *esprit de corps*, and believes strongly in military comradeship. In a sense his claim for 'esprit de Brigade' was a little far-fetched, for Battalions held to themselves very much, and the fact that they relieved each other, though often a bond of alliance, was sometimes also a cause of friction. Between Battalions he did not shrink from making comparisons. 'My Berks' had done this; 'My

Bucks' should do the same. Much good resulted. The standard of efficiency was raised. Though at times he was discovered to be naïvely inconsistent, one thing was certain—the 184th Brigade felt throughout its members that it was the best in the Division. The war has not produced many great men, but it has produced many great figures—amongst whom Robert White is by no means the least.

If it was well commanded by its General, the 184th Brigade was as well served by its staff. Gepp, the Brigade Major at Laventie, had been the pattern of a staff officer. His advice was at the service of the most recent company commander or newest subaltern. With Gepp as author, no march-table ever went wrong. Moore fell no whit short of his predecessor in ability. He was alike eager to acquire and to impart his knowledge, which in military matters was both profound and practical. He made friends readily with regimental officers, for he remained one of them at heart and in outlook. His powers were truly at the service of the whole Brigade. When George Moore left in September, 1917, to take command of a Battalion, the third Brigade Major who makes a figure in my history appeared—H. G. Howitt. In the sequence fortune continued to favour the Brigade. Howitt was a Territorial whose prowess had been proved in the Somme fighting. In place of a long staff training he brought business powers. He was indulgent of everything save fear, laziness, and inefficiency. Stout-hearted himself, he expected stoutness in others; this was the right attitude of a staff officer.

Though a business man by training, he did not negotiate with the war; in him everything was better than his writing.

Of these three, Gepp, Moore, Howitt, it would be difficult to name the best Brigade Major; the 184th Brigade was happy in the trio.

On November 9 the 2/4th Oxfords returned to the trenches in weather that was still relatively fine. The Brigade sector had been changed; its front now stretched across the Douai railway below the slope of Greenland Hill. The previous quietude of the trenches now gave place to more activity. German shelling much increased. The ruins of the famous Chemical Works, which covered several acres of ground, were daily stirred by the explosions of shells among the tangled wreckage of boiler-pipes and twisted metal. In the front line trench-mortaring became frequent. On November 14 Cuthbert was wounded by a bomb which fell inside the trench, and other casualties occurred, including the General's runner. Many new officers and men had joined since Ypres. Wiltshire took up the adjutantcy when Cuthbert left.

Plans were afoot for a big demonstration to cover the surprise by English tanks at Havrincourt on November 20. A series of gas projections, smoke barrages, and raids were to take place. The better to maintain secrecy from the German 'listening-sets' no telephones were used. The Battalion bore its share in the programme; already at Arras plans for a novel raid were under contemplation. Cuthbert had devised a scheme, which Colonel Wetherall adopted and chose B Company, under Moberly, to carry out. The details of this raid, inasmuch as their novelty is of some historical interest, demand an explanation.

Gas fired in shells was of two sorts, lethal and non-lethal. The former was a deadly poison. Unless taken in large quantities, the latter had no fatal, nor indeed serious, effects; designed to irritate the throat and eyes, it caused such sneezing and hiccoughing that whosoever breathed this sort of gas lost temporarily his self-control. Lethal and non-lethal gas were intermingled both by the Germans and ourselves with high explosive shells; the effect of each assisted the effect of the other. If one began to sneeze from the effect of non-lethal gas, one could not wear a gas-helmet to resist the lethal; the high-explosive shells disguised both types. Now it was planned by Wetherall to fire lethal gas against the enemy for several nights. On the night of the raid and during it, non-lethal only would be used. The two gases smelt alike and the presumption was that on the night of the raid the enemy would wear gas-helmets.

On the evening of November 17, only an hour before the raid was to take place, it was announced that the wrong type of shells had been delivered to the artillery. Barely in time to avert a fiasco, the affair was cancelled. Two nights afterwards, when the wind luckily was again from the right direction, the raid was carried out. The Germans, of whom some were found in gas-helmets, had no inkling of our plan. B Company, though they missed the gap through the enemy's wire, entered the trenches without opposition and captured a machine-gun

IN A GERMAN GUN-PIT NEAR GAVRELLE.

which was pointing directly at their approach but never fired. Wallington, the officer in command of the storming party, killed several Germans. As often, there was difficulty in finding the way back to our lines; in fact, Moberly, the commander of the raid, after some wandering in No-Man's-Land, entered the trenches of a Scotch division upon our right. His appearance and comparative inability to speak their language made him a suspicious visitor to our kilted neighbours. Moberly rejoined his countrymen under escort.

For a long time it seemed that no material results had been achieved in the raid. But the next morning Private Hatt, who for his exploit gained the D.C.M., crawled into our lines carrying the machine-gun which he had hugged all night between the German lines and ours. This raid took place the night preceding the great Cambrai offensive, and the success of Moberly and B Company formed part of the demonstration designed to attract enemy reserves away from the area of the operation mentioned.

On the last day of November the Division was withdrawn from the Arras sector; its move to relieve some of the troops who had been severely handled by the enemy at Bourlon Wood seemed probable. Events occurred to change the destination. The Battalion, after two nights at Arras, entrained amid all symptoms of haste on the morning of November 30 and travelled without the transport to Bapaume. The noise of battle and excited staff-officers greeted its arrival. In the back area it was on everybody's lips that the enemy had broken through. Bapaume was being shelled, many officers had travelled unprepared for an early engagement with the enemy, and the General was not yet on the scene; the situation was as unexpected as it was exciting. At 3 p.m. we were placed in 'buses under Bicknell's directions and moved rapidly to Bertincourt, a village four kilometres west of Havrincourt Wood. The night of November 30/December 1 was spent in an open field. It was intensely cold. At 4 a.m. a flank march was made to Fins, where some empty huts were found. Enemy long range shells, aimed at the railway, kept falling in the village. Through Fins at 10 a.m. on December 1 the Guards marched forward to do their famous counter-attack on Gouzeaucourt; on the afternoon of the same day the Battalion moved up to Metz, whither Brigade Headquarters had already gone. During the night, which was frosty and moonlight, the Colonel led the Battalion across country to occupy a part of the Hindenburgh Line west of La Vacquerie. On the following morning the enemy delivered a heavy attack upon the village, from which, after severe losses in killed and prisoners, troops of the 182nd Brigade were driven back. To assist them C Company was detached from the Battalion. The trenches—our front was now the Hindenburg Line—were frozen, there was snow on the ground, and the temporary supremacy of the enemy in guns and sniping produced a toll of casualties. It was an anxious time, but the Battalion was involved in no actual fighting; the German counter-attack, for the time-being, was at an end.

THE MOVE TO CAMBRAI, DECEMBER, 1917. 153

The 61st Division was left holding a line of snow-bound trenches between Gonnelieu and La Vacquerie, consisting of fragments both of the Hindenburg Line, the old German front line, and our own as it stood before the Cambrai battle opened. Except in the 184th Brigade the casualties suffered by the Division during the heavy German counter-attacks had been heavier than those at Ypres. The 2/4 Oxfords by luck had escaped a share in this fighting, and the Battalion's casualties during these critical events were few.

The German counter-attack from Cambrai was an important step in the war's progress. At the time it was considered even more important than it was. Judged by the rapidity with which they were replaced, the loss of guns and stores by us was not of high moment; it mattered more that for the first time since the Second Battle of Ypres the enemy had driven back our lines several miles. A counter-surprise had been effected. On a small scale the panic of defeat was proved by its physical results upon the ground. The valley north-east of Gouzeaucourt was littered with all kinds of relics, which in trench warfare or in our attacks had been unknown. Whole camps had been sacked and their contents, in the shape of clothing, equipment and blankets, were strewn broadcast. Packets of socks and shirts showed where an English quartermaster's stores had been, and flapping canvas and dismantled shelters were evidence of a local *débâcle* to our side. The sight of derelict tractors, motor cars, and steam rollers, left in the sunken road at Gouzeaucourt, produced a sense of shock.

A broad-gauge railway train, captured complete with trucks and locomotive and recovered in our counter-attack, bore witness to a victory seized but not secured. The battles of Ypres and Cambrai, 1917, though well-fought and not without results, robbed the British army for the time being of the initiative upon the Western Front. America became spoken of—1918, it was said, would be a defensive year. Yet the German success had in reality no effect upon our Infantry's morale. By the troops engaged in it Cambrai had been almost forgotten before Christmas. Less than a year afterwards the Germans had lost, not only Cambrai, but the war.

The end of 1917 was as cold as its beginning. Snow and frost, destined to play utter havoc with the roads, laid their white mantle on the battlefield. Fighting had slackened when the Battalion went into the line in front of Gonnelieu. The trenches there ran oddly between derelict tanks, light railways, and dismantled huts; in No-Man's-Land lay several batteries of our guns.

On December 7 the 183rd Brigade relieved the Battalion, which moved back to tents in Havrincourt Wood. It was bitter! Shells and aeroplane bombs made the wood dangerous as well as cold. On the 10th a further tour in the front line commenced. This time trenches north-east of Villers Plouich were held. Wiring was strenuously carried out, but save for activity by trench-mortars the enemy lay quiet. The Battalion returned to Havrincourt Wood on December 15 and remained in its frozen tents until the Division was relieved by the 63rd. After one night at Lechelle the Bat-

THE CANAL DU NORD AT YTRES.

talion entrained at Ytres and moved back to Christmas rest-billets at Suzanne, near Bray.

Huts, built by the French but vacated more than a year ago and now very dilapidated, formed the accommodation. In them Christmas dinners, to procure which Bennett had proceeded early from the line, were eaten. And O'Meara conducted the Brigade band.

CHAPTER XIII.

THE GREAT GERMAN ATTACK OF MARCH 21.

JANUARY, FEBRUARY, MARCH, 1918.

The French relieved on the St. Quentin front.—The calm before the storm.—A golden age.—The Warwick raid.—The German attack launched.—Defence of Enghien Redoubt.—Counter-attack by the Royal Berks.—Holnon Wood lost.—The battle for the Beauvoir line.—The enemy breaks through.

THE Battalion's mid-winter respite was brief. On New Year's Eve, 1917, the 2/4th Oxfords quitted the wretched Suzanne huts and marched through Harbonnières to Caix. No 'march past' was necessary or would have been possible, for so slippery was the road that the men had to trail along its untrodden sides as best they could. Old 61st Divisional sign-boards left standing nearly a year ago greeted the return to an area which was familiar to many. The destination should have been Vauvillers, but the inhabitants of that village were stricken with measles. Better billets and freedom from infection compensated for a longer march. At Caix the Battalion was comfortable for a week.

THE GREAT GERMAN ATTACK OF MARCH 21, 1918.

The Division's move from the Bray-Suzanne area to south of the Somme heralded a new relief of the French, whose line was now to be shortened by the amount on its left flank between St. Quentin and La Fère. About January 11 the Battalion found itself once more in Holnon Wood, where a large number of huts and dug-outs had been made by the French since last spring. The front line, now about to be held between Fayet and Gricourt, was almost in its old position. The outpost line of nine months ago had crystallised into the usual trench system. Those courteous preliminaries, so much the feature of a French relief, were, on this re-introduction to scenes soon to become so famous —and so tragic—a little marred by an untimely German shell which wounded Weller, who had accompanied the Colonel to see the new line.

Industrious calm succeeded the relief. Since the Russian break-up and the consequent liberation from the Eastern Front of fresh German legions, the British army had been on the defensive. A big effort by the enemy was expected, and when it came, the St. Quentin front was not unlikely to receive the brunt of his massed attack. The months of January and February and the first half of March were ominously quiet. Shelling was spasmodic. After the artillery activity of the last summer and autumn our guns seemed lazy. So quiet was it that Abraham used to ride up to the two small copses that lay behind our front.

For the time being the 'offensive spirit' was in abeyance; our paramount task was the perfection of our defensive system. By this time in the war it was acknowledged that against attacks in weight no actual line could be held intact. Faith in 'lines' became qualified in favour of the series of 'strong points' or redoubts, which were constructed to defend 'tactical features.' This policy, founded on our experience of the German defence during the Third Battle of Ypres, was very sound. All the redoubts constructed in the area occupied by the 184th Brigade were so well sited and so strongly wired that the faith seemed justified that they were part of one impregnable system. But against loss of one important factor no amount of industry could serve to insure. 'Strong points' must act in concert and for such mutual action 'on the day' good visibility was essential. As we shall see, this factor was denied. In rear of these redoubts, which lay along the ridge west of Fayet, a line known as the 'Battle Line' was fortified, and in rear again a trench was dug to mark the 'Army Line,' where the last stand would be made. These lines were strong, but more reliance was apt to be placed upon their mere existence on the ground than, in default of any co-existent scheme to fill them at a crisis with appropriate garrisons, was altogether justified.[1]

Early in the year the Bucks had been taken from the Brigade (now like all Infantry Brigades reduced to three Battalions) and went to Nesle to work as an entrenching Battalion. Many old friends, including especially Colonel 'Jock' Muir, had to be parted with. The three Battalions which remained were now arranged in 'depth,' a phrase

[1] For the *terrain* referred to in this chapter see the maps ante pp. 83 and 95.

explained by stating that while one, say the Berks, held the front line 'twixt Fayet and Gricourt, the Gloucesters as Support Battalion would be in Holnon Wood and ourselves, the Oxfords, in reserve and back at Ugny. When a relief took place the Gloucesters went to the front line, ourselves to Holnon, and the Berks back to Ugny. The Battalion holding the line was similarly disposed in 'depth,' for its headquarters and one company were placed more than a mile behind the actual front.

After the January frost and snow had gone, a period of fine, clement weather set in. This, in a military sense, was a golden age. Boxing, thanks to encouragement from the Colonel and Brown and under the practical doctrine of 'Benny' Thomas, the Battalion pugilist, flourished as never before. Each tour some officers, instead of going to the line, were sent to worship at the shrine of Maxse. The Battalion reached the zenith of its efficiency. Early in March some reinforcements from the 6th Oxfords, who had been disbanded, arrived; they numbered two hundred. Among the new officers who joined were Foreshew, Rowbotham, and Cunningham. Foreshew received command of C Company, whose commander Matthews went to England for a six months' rest. To Hobbs also, our worthy quartermaster, it was necessary to bid a reluctant farewell. His successor, Murray, a very able officer from the 4th Gloucesters, arrived in time to check the table of stores before the opening of the great offensive.

On the night of 18/19 March the Battalion went into the front line. C Company was on the right, in front of Fayet; B Company, under the command of Wallington, was on the left, just south of Gricourt. A went to Fayet itself and D Company, commanded in Robinson's absence by Rowbotham, provided the garrison of Enghien Redoubt, which was a quarry near Selency Château; Battalion Headquarters also were at this redoubt. During the night of March 20 a raid on the Battalion's right was carried out near Cepy Farm by the 182nd Brigade. It was successful. German prisoners from three divisions corroborated our suspicion that the great enemy offensive was about to be launched. From headquarters to headquarters throbbed the order to man battle stations. Ere dawn was due to lighten the sky a dense mist shrouded everything and added a fresh factor to the suspense.

Early on March 21, only a short time after the Colonel had returned from visiting the front line posts, the ground shook to a mighty bombardment. At Amiens windows rattled in their frames. Trench mortars of all calibres and field guns, brought to closest range in the mist and darkness, began to pound a pathway through our wire. Back in artillery dug-outs the light of matches showed the time; it was 4.50 a.m. The hour had struck. Our guns, whose programme in reply was the fruit of two months' preparation, made a peculiar echo as their shells crackled through the mist. Some 'silent' guns[1] fired for the first time.

---

[1] Defensive artillery, whose inactivity prior to the German attack was intended to ensure against discovery by enemy sound-rangers and observers.

On all headquarters, roads, redoubts, and observation posts the enemy's howitzer shells were falling with descending swoop, and battery positions were drenched with gas.

In the back area the fire of long-range guns was brought with uncanny accuracy to bear against our rest billets, transport lines, and dumps. Cross-roads, bridges, and all vital spots in our communications, though never previously shelled, were receiving direct hits within a short time of the opening of the bombardment. The Berks had casualties at Ugny. Some English heavy batteries, recent arrivals on the front and seemingly undiscovered by the enemy, were now knocked out almost as soon as they had opened fire. The Attilly level crossing was hit by an early shell which blocked the road there with a huge crater. Never in the war had the Germans flung their shells so far or furiously as now.

By daylight all front line wire had been destroyed, and our trenches everywhere were much damaged. The mist hung thick, but the Germans did not yet attack. About 9.30 a.m. the barrage was felt to lift westwards from Fayet and the fitful clatter of Lewis guns, firing in short bursts with sometimes a long one exhausting a 'drum,' was heard. In the front line showers of stick bombs announced the enemy's presence. Everywhere it seemed that quick-moving bodies in grey uniforms were closing in from either flank and were behind. In the mist our posts were soon over-run. Few of our men were left to rally at the 'keeps.' A messenger to A Company's platoons, which had been stationed in support at the famous 'Sunken Road,' found that place filled with Germans. Before noon the enemy had passed Fayet and his patrols had reached Selency and the Cottages.

At Enghien Redoubt Battalion Headquarters had received no news of the attack having begun; the dense mist limited the view to fifty yards. The earliest intimation received by Colonel Wetherall of what was taking place was enemy rifle and machine-gun fire sweeping the parapet. At one corner of the redoubt some of the enemy broke in but were driven out by D Company with the bayonet. Outside Headquarters the first three men to put their heads over were killed by Germans, who had crept close along the sunken road which leads from Fayet to Selency Château. The rifles and machine guns of the garrison opened up and gained superiority. The defence, destined to last for many hours, of Enghien Redoubt proved an important check to the enemy's advance and helped to save many of our guns.

At 12 noon, after several patrols had failed to find out whether the enemy had captured Holnon, the Colonel himself went out to see all that was happening. He did not return, and shortly afterwards Headquarters were surrounded by the enemy, who had made ground on either flank. Nevertheless till 4.30 p.m. Cunningham, the officer left in command, held out most manfully. Of all the companies, Jones and less than fifty men had escaped capture. They reached the 'Battle Line' of trenches east of Holnon Wood, and there joined the Gloucesters, who had not yet been engaged in the fighting. The enemy, having captured Maissemy, Fayet, and Holnon, paused to reorganise as evening fell.

Towards evening on the 21st the Berks, who were in reserve when the attack started, were sent to counter-attack against Maissemy, which had been lost by the division on our left. Near the windmill, which stands on the high ground west of the village, Dimmer, the Berks V.C. Colonel, was killed leading his men on horseback. This local attempt to stem the German onslaught proved of no avail. At 10.30 a.m. on March 22 the enemy, whose movements were again covered by mist, pressed the attack against the Battle Line. Almost before the Gloucesters knew they were attacked in front, they found themselves beset in flanks and rear.

At noon the enemy from its north side had penetrated Holnon Wood. Gloucesters and Oxfords fell back to join the garrison of the Beauvoir Line, all parts of which were heavily engaged by evening. A gallant resistance, in which the Gloucesters under Colonel Lawson were specially distinguished, was made by the 184th Infantry Brigade. The General encouraged the defence in person. But the line was too weakly manned long to withstand the enemy; though parts of it held till after 8 p.m. on March 22, before midnight the whole of this last Army Line had been lost. The enemy had 'broken through.'

CHAPTER XIV.

THE BRITISH RETREAT,

MARCH, 1918.

Rear-guard actions.—The Somme crossings.—Bennett relieved by the 20th Division at Voyennes.—Davenport with mixed troops ordered to counter-attack at Ham.—Davenport killed.—The enemy crosses the Somme.—The stand by the 184th Infantry Brigade at Nesle.—Colonel Wetherall wounded.—Counter-attack against La Motte.—Bennett captured.—The Battalion's sacrifice in the great battle.

AFTER the battle for the Beauvoir Line the 184th Infantry Brigade was ordered back to Nesle. At Languevoisin on March 23 we find the relics of the 2/4th Oxfords under the command of Major Bennett, who with a force including other members of the Battalion had been providing rearguards at the crossings of the Somme. What force was this? To understand the story it is necessary to go back a little and see what had been happening behind the line since March 21.

When the attack was known to have commenced, all transport, quartermasters' stores, and men left out of the line were ordered back to Ugny, where Bennett as senior Major present formed all our divisional details into a composite Battalion some 900 strong. Early on March 22 Colonel Wetherall, limping and tired, arrived. He bore the tale of his adventure. During the 21st we saw him disappear from Enghien Redoubt to go on a reconnaissance. Near Holnon he was surrounded by an enemy patrol and led a prisoner towards St. Quentin; but when the fire of 6-inch howitzers scared his escort into shell-holes, the Colonel escaped, and the same night, choosing his opportunity to slip between the German digging parties, contrived to reach our lines.

As March 22 lengthened out, the tide of battle rolled nearer and nearer towards Ugny, above which air fighting at only a few hundred feet from the ground was taking place. At 7 p.m. Bennett had orders to move his men westwards across the Somme. Soon afterwards a runner came posthaste. He told of the fighting on the Beauvoir line; the intrepid General had been wounded in the head while with his shrapnel helmet in his hand he waved encouragement to his men. Colonel Wetherall had already started on the way to Languevoisin but was caught up at Matigny. He the same night (22nd) regained the Beauvoir line and took command of the Brigade. As we have seen, he moved back with the Brigade on the next day.

Further developments soon diverted Bennett's force, whose fortunes we are following. At Matigny he was ordered by the Major-General with half his force to guard the Offoy bridgehead and with the other half to hold Voyennes. The Offoy garrison was despatched under Moberly, who was commanding the details of the 184th Brigade, including a hundred Oxfords. Moberly's force comprised many administrative personnel. 'What your men lack in numbers they must make up in courage,' was the Major-General's encouragement.

But the men were not at once put to the test. The 20th Division, which was covering the retreat across the Somme, relieved the Offoy rear-guard, of which Davenport had now assumed command, early in the morning of March 23, and Bennett was likewise relieved in his duties at Voyennes, where the bridge was blown up. Though the Offoy bridgehead had been taken over by the 20th Division, Davenport's troops were kept in support along the railway embankment at Hombleux, for it was feared that the enemy had already commenced to cross the Somme at Ham. During the morning of the 23rd Davenport received peremptory orders to make a counter-attack against the town with the object of regaining possession of its bridgehead. Considerable success resulted; Verlaines was cleared of the enemy's patrols, and the advance reached the ridge east of that village.

With fresh troops acting on a concerted plan something might have been accomplished. Davenport's men were a disorganised mixture of many battalions, including, besides the Oxfords and other representatives of the 184th Brigade, a number of Cornwalls and King's Liverpools. They were unfed, and the demoralisation of the retreat was beginning to do its work. As always on these occasions, when officers of different services were thrown together, divided counsels were the result. Moberly, an officer who could have been relied upon to make the best of the situation, was wounded

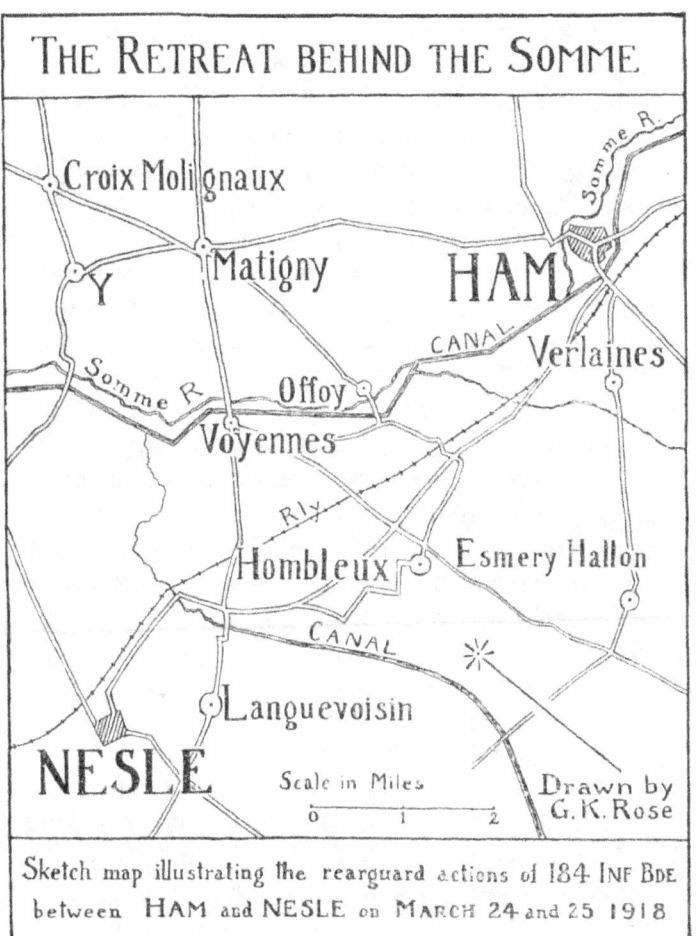

in the leg during a moonlight reconnaissance with Davenport.

By March 24 the position was unaltered; the troops were still lining the ridge east of Verlaines and awaited the enemy's next move with their field of fire in many cases masked by, or masking, that of their comrades. Against this type of defence the enemy's tactics did not require to be as infallible as they perhaps seemed. Our pity is drawn to these English troops, disorganised, without their own proper commanders, unsupplied with rations—the stop-gaps thrust forward in the last stages of a retreat.

At 9 a.m. the enemy, whose patrols had during the night of March 23/24 been feeling their way up the slopes from the Somme Canal, commenced to press forward in earnest. The mixed troops, who were lining the ridge, had been 'down' too long to offer much resistance. They melted away, as leaderless troops will. Davenport, a gallant officer who to the very last never spared himself, was killed, shot through the head at Verlaines. The enemy, whose advanced artillery was already in action from behind Ham, had secured Esmery Hallon by the evening. Nesle was threatened.

On the same day of which I was last speaking —March 24—the 184th Brigade, minus those Oxfords who were in action with the 20th Division, though sadly wasted in numbers, formed up again to make a stand. Colonel Wetherall, the acting Brigadier, had received orders to hold the line of the Canal east and south-east of Nesle. On the left of this line stood the Oxfords under Bennett,

LIEUT.-COL. H. E. DE R. WETHERALL,
D.S.O., M.C.

200 Berks under Willink were in the centre, while the Gloucesters, about 120 strong under Colonel Lawson, guarded the right. At 11 a.m. on March 25 the enemy attacked. As often during these days, when a line was held solidly in one place, it broke elsewhere. By noon the enemy had captured Nesle, and the left flank of the Brigade was turned. During the fight Colonel Wetherall was wounded in the neck by a piece of shell and owed his life to the Brigade Major, Howitt, who held the arteries.

The line was driven back to Billancourt and the same night (25th) the remnants of the XVIII Corps withdrew in darkness to Roye, a town where our hospitals were still at work, evacuating as fast as possible the streams of wounded from the battle. One of the last patients to leave by train was Wetherall, who at this crisis passed under the care of Stobie, the Oxfords' old M.O.

On March 26 we see the 184th Brigade held in reserve near Mezières, to be suddenly moved at midnight of March 27/28 by lorries. The lorries made towards Amiens, and it appeared that the battered relics of the Brigade were being withdrawn. The belief was disappointed. At Villers Bretonneux Bennett received orders from a staff officer to go to Marcelçave, where the 61st Division was being concentrated for a counter-attack at dawn against the village of La Motte. In the darkness the route was missed and the convoy drove straight into our front line. Marcelçave was reached eventually, but so late that a dawn attack was impossible. At 10 a.m. on March 28 the forlorn enterprise, in which the 183rd Brigade, the

Gloucesters, and the Berks shared, was launched from the station yard. The troops were footsore, sleepless, and unfed. They were mostly men from regimental employ—pioneers, clerks, storemen—to send whom forward across strange country to drive the enemy from the village he had seized on the important Amiens—St. Quentin road was a mockery. Such efforts at counter-attack resulted in more and more ground being lost. Still, the men staggered forward bravely, to come almost at once under fierce enfilade machine-gun fire. The losses were heavy. Craddock, a young officer now serving under Bennett, moved about among the men, encouraging them by his example of coolness and gallantry.

When 350 yards short of La Motte the advance was driven to take cover. It was useless to press on; in fact, already there was real danger of being surrounded. Bennett, whose leadership thoughout was excellent, with difficulty extricated his men by doubling them in two's across the open. Towards evening those that got back were placed in trenches outside Marcelçave.

By now that village was being severely shelled and bombed, and in danger of becoming surrounded by the enemy. Soon after dark it was attacked in earnest. Bennett stayed too long in Marcelçave attempting to get news of the situation and some orders. Brigade Headquarters had in fact already left, before Bennett, instead of returning to his former headquarters, decided to join his men in the trenches before the village. Those trenches were no longer being fought for. Near the railway bridge he ran straight into the enemy as they swarmed towards the village and was captured. The remains of the Battalion were driven back on Villers Bretonneux, the contents of which village had to make up for absent rations. Robinson, who had returned from leave in time to take part in the La Motte affair, assumed command. The Australians were at hand; fresh troops arrived to relieve those worn out by a week's continuous fighting. After four days at Gentelles all that were left of the 2/4th Oxfords, together with the other fragments of the 61st Division, were withdrawn for rest and reorganisation west of Amiens.

A Battalion is too small for its historian to enter into any controversy upon the measures taken for the defence of the St. Quentin front. Whatever else the Oxfords could have done would have had no effect upon the main issues of this great attack. But for the mist the German onslaught, delivered in the preponderance of four to one, would hardly have achieved the same historical result. The Battalion had stood in the forefront of the greatest battle of the war. Accounts, already growing legendary, tell how our men acquitted themselves that day. Some posts fought on till all were killed or wounded. There were few stragglers. Of B Company, only one man returned from the front line. It is said of A Company that, when surrounded by the enemy, Brown formed the men into a circle, back to back, and fought without surrender.

The monument which stands above Fayet is happily placed. It is inscribed to the sons of France who fell in action nearly fifty years ago.

On March 21, 1918, it was enriched by its association with a later sacrifice. The credit won in this lost battle gives to the 2/4th Oxford and Bucks Light Infantry a share of honour in the war equal to that which has been earned by our most successful troops in the advance.

The loss in all ranks had been so heavy that the killed and missing could only be computed by counting over those few that remained. Bennett and all four company commanders in the line were missing. The Colonel and Moberly had been sent to England wounded. Jones was the only officer from the front line who remained safe. Cairns, the Sergeant-Major of A Company, had come through and earned distinction. The loss in Lewis gunners, signallers, and runners had been especially heavy. Douglas, the Regimental Sergeant-Major, after most valuable work in the Battalion, had been killed. Transport and stores, for extricating which credit was due to Abraham and Murray, alone came out complete.

Chapter XV.

THE BATTLE OF THE LYS,

April—May, 1918.

Effects of the German offensive.—The Battalion amalgamated with the Bucks.—Entrainment for the Merville area.—A dramatic journey.—The enemy break-through on the Lys.—The Battalion marches into action.—The defence of Robecq.—Operations of April 12, 13, 14.—The fight for Baquerolle Farm.—A troublesome flank.—Billeted in St. Venant.—The lunatic asylum.—La Pierrière.—The Robecq sector.

THE closing phases of the war are so comparatively fresh and vividly remembered that a less close description need be attempted of them than of more early periods. I feel that justice cannot easily be done to the events of last year, events which in dramatic force eclipsed any since the Battle of the Marne. Of 1918, moreover, the facts have not yet had time to drop into that relief which a historian prefers before reducing them to chronicle. It is unlikely that, in years hence, when the full history of the war is written, the German offensive of 1918 will not be taken as the turning point in the great conflict. For the second time since the invasion of Belgium and for the first since conscription, readers of the *Times* saw a black line sagging across the map towards the English Channel. In France at the end of March conditions meriting the popular description of 'wind up' were recognisable. Bases were crowded to overflowing. Train services were seriously deranged by the German approach to Amiens. The traffic upon the main roads in the Somme valley was an eloquent intermingling of troops, guns, and civilians evacuating as much of their property as possible upon wagons and carts, which were piled high with children, tables, utensils, bedsteads, farm implements, and always mattresses. The shelling of Amiens Cathedral and the long gun which played on Paris were signs of the destructive ascendancy of the enemy. Our railways, which depended on a few junctions now placed none too far behind the line, were attacked vigorously by the enemy in the hope of their disorganisation. St. Pol station was shelled to ruins; Hazebrouck, Chocques, and Doullens were nightly targets for German bombs. Already at Tinques and Achiet the R.T.O.s had been killed. (We had done the same and more to the Germans for two years). Our railwaymen and engine drivers showed staunch devotion to duty and were as much responsible as any branch of the service for keeping our armies fighting during the critical months of the spring and early summer.

To Avesne, a remote village behind Amiens, the 2/4th Oxfords were withdrawn early in April for completion with new drafts and for refitting. An amalgamation—which was a great advantage to both units—of the Battalion with the Bucks now took place. As the 25th Entrenching Battalion the Bucks had been engaged in the fighting round

Nesle, when they became attached to a Brigade of the 20th Division. They were now most anxious to be sent to join us or at all events to rejoin the 61st Division. Unable to obtain the orders they desired, the Bucks availed themselves of the prevailing confusion to march away 'without authority' and were already at Avesne when the Oxfords arrived.

The addition of some 300 N.C.O.s and men, with whom came such valued officers as Clutsom, Buttfield, Kemp, Lodge, Boase, Kirk, and several others, acted as an infusion of new blood and vigour into the Battalion which had given nearly all of its best in the St. Quentin fighting. As the senior officer now present, I was placed in command of the Battalion after the amalgamation, for which no more suitable surroundings could have been found than Avesne, whose château and grounds we had to ourselves. On April 7, before the regimental tailors had half finished substituting the red circles for the black ones previously carried by the Bucks, a large draft of 431 men joined the Battalion from England. Many of these were boys, but among them stood a few veteran soldiers who had been out before and been wounded. With this draft, which I believe was posted without the knowledge that the Bucks had joined us, the Battalion reached the strength of over 1,000 men. It was a goodly force, unhampered by passengers. With Abraham, Murray, and Regimental Sergeant-Major Hedley (from the Bucks) those departments of the Battalion not purely tactical were sure to be well managed. I felt quite confident in the command of this force of men, and General Pagan, the new Brigadier, was kind enough to express his confidence in my ability.

Our billets at Avesne—the entire Battalion was accommodated in the buildings of a large château from which some army school had been precipitated by the German advance—were too good for much hope to be entertained of a long stay in them. The unified command from now onwards brought more rapid moves than formerly had been the custom. Thus at a few hours' notice 'billeting parties' were ordered, not back towards Amiens, but to Merville and St. Venant. The 61st was to become a Division in G.H.Q. reserve behind the old Laventie sector. But before Battalions could follow their representatives and while the billeting was still in progress the Germans attacked and broke through on the Lys, south of Armentières. We marched, however, from Avesne on April 11 in happy ignorance of this new battle. Not till Hangest, and there by means of a Continental *Daily Mail*, was the changed prospect of our destination revealed. The Hangest R.T.O. was half beside himself with excitement and delay. There were several hours to spend in waiting, and during this time the kits were retrieved from the station yard and a prudent change was made from soft hats into shrapnel helmets and fighting equipment. After a rapid entrainment we at last pulled out at about 2 p.m. So strong was the Battalion that D Company, which itself numbered over 200, was unable to travel with us and had to follow by a later train. In its early stages the journey, though similar to most of the

THE BATTLE OF THE LYS, APRIL—MAY, 1918. 177

kind, produced one formidable incident, for at the top of the steep gradient between Candas and Doullens the train snapped in half; its hind portion was left poised in a cutting for an hour, until two locomotives arrived to push it on to Doullens, whither the forward half, in gay ignorance, had run.

The night was overcast, a fact which doubtless saved us from the attention of enemy aeroplanes. The journey from St. Pol through Chocques and Lillers to Steenbecque is stamped on the memory by its more than many halts, the occasional glare of mines and munition factories which, in anticipation of another break-through, seemed to be working at tensest pressure to evacuate coal and manufactured stores from capture by the enemy; by the loud booming of artillery, to which the train seemed to draw specially near at Chocques and Isbergues; and the final sudden grinding of the brakes at Steenbecque, distracted railwaymen, and the small hut in which Bennett and the Brigade Staff were exhibiting a mixture of excitement, impatience and a sort of reckless familiarity with this apparent repetition of the Somme retreat. At Steenbecque station, which is three miles short of Hazebrouck and hidden behind the Nieppe Forest, we received the latest news of the battle into which we were being so dramatically plunged: the enemy had broken through the feeble resistance of the Portuguese and was outside Merville. My orders were to take up a line, which was at present covered by the 51st Division, between Robecq and Calonne and for that object to detrain and move forward immediately. The station yard was ill-suited to a rapid detrainment, there being few ramps or sidings, and despite the impatience of Bennett, a Divisional Staff Officer, who was most anxious to get finished before dawn, we were kept seated in the train for nearly two hours. This delay was really most valuable, for it enabled me to appreciate the situation and issue detailed orders, which otherwise it would never have been possible to give.

As the dawn of April 12, 1918, was breaking, we set foot to the long pavé road which runs through the Nieppe Forest to St. Venant, followed by the transport and the cookers, from which at the cost of never so much delay I felt determined to give the men, who had had no proper meal for twenty-four hours, a good square feed before becoming involved in the uncertain and possibly rationless conflict which lay before us in country that was likely to have been looted by the retreating Portuguese. Nevertheless, during this breakfast, taken at the eastern edge of the great Forest of Nieppe, feverish messages arrived, which said that the enemy was in Robecq and already crossing the La Bassée Canal. This, of course, was not true, but troops who are moving up towards an advancing enemy, though met by exaggerated and conflicting reports of the hostile progress, are almost confined, until actual encounter occurs, to this species of information. By now Corps Headquarters, after a three years' sojourn at Hinges, had commenced to scour the country west of Aire for a suitably remote château. Except for Howitt there was no staff officer upon the spot, and we found after passing St. Venant towards Robecq that it was every man for himself in the task of stemming the German attack. Parts of the Division, notably the 5th D.C.L.I. and the 2/6th Warwicks, which had been detrained earlier than ourselves to join in the battle, had been roughly handled in fighting south of Merville during the night of April 11/12. The 51st Division was to all intents out of action, and there was a gap of more than a mile between Robecq and Calonne on the morning of April 12. Into, but not through, this gap German patrols had penetrated, and at Carvin had crossed the streams Noc and Clarence. As a matter of fact these enemy were but the flankers of an advanced guard, whose objective at this time lay in the direction of Haverskerque. Thus it befell that the Battalion came into no direct conflict with the main enemy forces on April 12.

Still the situation at 9 a.m. was both obscure and difficult. Until their ammunition seemed to be expended, our artillery, which had withdrawn behind the La Bassée Canal, kept up a fire upon the open ground between Les Amusoires, where the Battalion was concentrating, and the Calonne road, which it was necessary for us to cross. Doubtless this untoward shelling was due to the reports spread by stragglers, of whom there was a considerable number from different units. Shortly after this occurrence I had the good fortune to meet a gunner subaltern, and for the next few days, pending a reinforcement of the artillery, what guns there were gave us excellent support. A greater menace came from the long dumps of our shells north of Robecq cemetery, to which some irresponsible person had

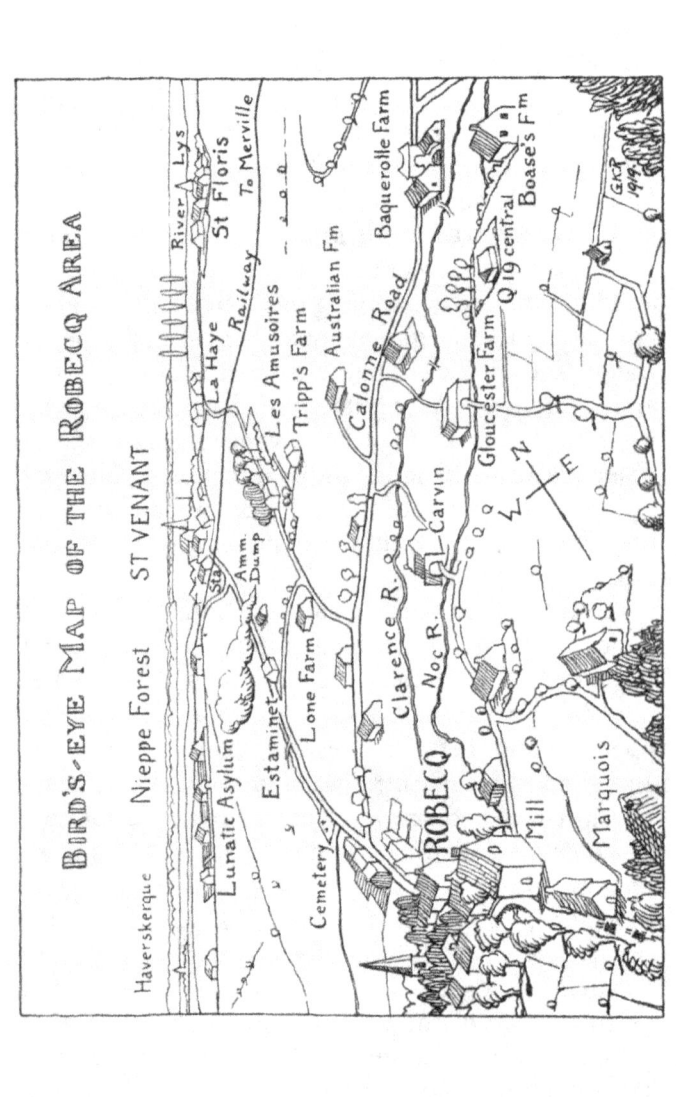

set fire. An acre of explosives was ablaze, barring progress across a wide area. Later a fusilade of small-arms ammunition broke out near St. Venant station, suggestive of fighting in our rear. There also it had been the final errand of some dump-keeper, in a fancied performance of duty, to destroy ammunition of which there was a crying need. Subsequently St. Venant was quite heavily bombed by our own aircraft—an example of what could happen during the time that our higher organisation was out of gear.

The appearance of the Battalion, which could easily have passed for a Brigade of Infantry as it issued, about 10 a.m., from among the trees of Les Amusoires, may have been a moral factor in itself sufficient to indispose the German outposts to remain longer upon the outskirts of Robecq. From my former knowledge of the ground I decided to use no delay in occupying the network of orchards and as many of the farms as possible along the Calonne road before hostile opposition increased. After sharp fighting and some 30 casualties, mostly in C Company, which was on the left, a line was reached beyond Noc river, between Robecq and Calonne. On the right we linked up with the Berks (who placed their headquarters in the estaminet at Robecq cross-roads) and on the left with the 2/7th Warwicks, whose line bent back at a right angle across the Calonne road towards La Haye. During the afternoon fighting for the possession of Baquerolle Farm and its adjacent orchards engaged the Battalion's left flank. In this fighting Lodge, a young officer to whom command of C Company had fallen in consequence of a wound to Captain Buttfield, and also Boase much distinguished themselves. To them and to the N.C.O.s of C Company, and also to the conduct of the new draft, was owing the success of the day's operations. By 3 p.m. not only had the Battalion accomplished the task assigned to it twenty-four hours previously, when the extent of the German advance was unknown, but ground was being made and the enemy was being driven backward upon Calonne. Robecq was guaranteed.

All day very severe fighting was in progress a mile to our left. Merville and Calonne were almost blotted out in smoke, and the air was thronged with aeroplanes. The heap of shells behind us still burned. By now the clouds which rose from this bonfire had become such a pall in the sky that the German balloons—the enemy was expert in moving forward this machinery of observation—could see nothing of the surrounding country. The Robecq district was remarkable for its well-stocked farms, and with the general flight of the civilians large numbers of unmilked cows, geese, goats, hens, and all manner of farmyard creatures commenced to stray across the fields and down the roads. Battalion Headquarters, which were ultimately established at a large farmhouse in Les Amusoires, as dusk approached, seemed to become the rendezvous for lowing cattle, hens, pigs, goats, and small armies of geese, to manage all of which a certain number of cowherds and farm-hands had to be detailed. Nor was it only at Battalion Headquarters that these movable larders were in the process of congregation.

At nightfall, when the companies—D Company

had rejoined during the afternoon—were settled into a secure outpost position and the Brigadier (General Pagan) had visited and approved the dispositions, an order from Corps was received to retreat a mile and to dig trenches across the open, hedgeless fields which stretched between Robecq and St. Venant. The whole of the Calonne road was to be abandoned. It was difficult to account for such a policy, which meant, not only the relinquishment of two bridge-heads of some importance and numerous farms and orchards which had been carried at expense and since garrisoned to good purpose, but the adoption instead of a position in rear, which was condemned with every tactical disadvantage and in which it would be impossible to remain once the enemy had secured possession of the ground we were now ordered to give up. I am happy to say that these orders, which can only have emanated from some staff inadequately informed upon the situation, were cancelled during the night and before the Battalion had acted on them. The fact is, I expressly remained in the forward position until at least rations had been delivered to the men, and by the time that had been done the staff pendulum had swung again. The salient of Baquerolle Farm, which it had cost valuable lives to reach, was retained.

On the morning of April 13 the enemy, under cover of a dense mist, which allowed his use of close-range artillery, attacked St. Floris, in front of which the Gloucesters were stationed. A demonstration against the Battalion accompanied, and in the mist it was uncertain whether an enemy attack on Robecq were not developing. The attack died down without the Germans having penetrated the Gloucesters, who put up a stout defence. Our line elsewhere was firm.

On the next day it was decided to use an opportunity to improve the position of our outpost line by occupying a group of cottages which lay in front. A platoon of A Company practically reached the nearest cottages without a sign of hostile opposition being shown. The fate of this little operation was the fruit of my miscalculation of the enemy's strength. The Germans knew better than ourselves how to sit still behind their machine-guns and avoid discovery. French civilians were moving about among the cottages at the time when our advance to occupy them was made and it seemed impossible that the enemy could be holding them even weakly. Civilians, too, were mingled in the fray as well on this as on later occasions. After trench-warfare days there was an incongruity in some episodes, which was not devoid of humour. One old Frenchman, at an hour when his farm was actually being fought over, arrived at Company Headquarters with a special pass-port to feed his beasts; and the tenacity of an old woman in clinging to her household gods terminated in her discovery, at the time of an attack, in a shell-hole in No-Man's-Land, where she was sheltering from the machine-gun barrage under a large umbrella (one felt that she at least deserved a copy of the operation orders!) During the ensuing weeks visits by French civilians to the front line became such that almost as many sentries were required to watch or

restrain their movements as were needed against the enemy.

A more serious attack, in which the 4th Division upon our right was intended to co-operate, was made by B Company at 7.30 p.m. on April 15 against the same cottages, which formed part of the hamlet called La Pierre au Beurre. Our bombardment in support of this attack was almost due to start, when an urgent message from the line announced that large forces of the enemy were massing opposite our front. To have called for S.O.S. fire by the artillery would totally have upset the programme of attack, and one could only hope that our zero would be the earlier. Luck was in our favour. Whatever else happened that night, it is certain that the enemy received a severe shelling from our guns.

The attack, carried out by B Company under Stanley, with D in support, was quite successful in its plan but not in its result. From a cause such as every series of complicated operations in open warfare threatened to introduce, the troops of the 4th Division on our right failed to co-operate as we expected. O'Meara, whom Stanley had placed in charge of his leading troops, after securing the cottages named as his objective, found himself attacked by the enemy from the very direction whence he had counted on assistance. After ineffectual attempts by our 'liaison' officer, Kirk, to get our neighbours to do their share, B Company had to be withdrawn to their original position. The 4th Division at this time were the flank division of one corps while we were of another. To reach the

Battalion acting on our right a notice of our plan had to climb up through our Brigade, Division, and Corps to Army and down again as many steps the other side. A staff-officer from Army or from Corps should have been on the spot.

Coucher and Kemp, two capital officers, were killed during the evening when this attack took place. Our other casualties were Killed, 2; Wounded, 18; Missing, 1.

Throughout April 13 and for several days afterwards desultory fighting, in which our trench-mortars under Miller performed good service, was maintained for the possession of Baquerolle Farm and another lying 150 yards south of it and christened Boase's Farm. Both remained in our hands. With the troops on our left flank there was some difficulty. Their line bent back awkwardly, and when the enemy shelled the houses on the Calonne road, where their right flank rested, they showed signs of withdrawing and leaving our C Company 'in the air.' The Germans quickly benefited by this irresolution, for they commenced to push forward from house to house along the Calonne road, until Baquerolle Farm was in danger of being taken in its rear. The prompt determination of Lodge, the officer I have already mentioned as commanding C Company, served to avert critical consequences. He delivered a local counter-attack, capturing a machine-gun and killing several of the enemy. Our neighbours thus reoccupied their former positions, but were warned in Divisional Orders not to give up any more of the Robecq-Calonne road. This incident, which rightly earned for 'Tommy' Lodge a Military Cross, had a vexatious sequel a few days later. In quoting where the left flank of the Battalion in fact rested I made a slip in the co-ordinates of its map reference. By that mistake I was trapped, when it appeared as black and white in relief orders, into having to hand over 100 yards of extra frontage, and had the mortification of causing several hours of troublesome delay to the front line, besides innocently saddling my successors with responsibility that was not honestly theirs to receive.

By April 16 the tactical situation was already stable. On that night—in reality during the early hours of April 17—the Battalion was relieved almost in the ordinary way by the Gloucesters, who came forward from the luxury of St. Venant and took over the line between Carvin and Baquerolle. St. Venant had been Portuguese G.H.Q. but was so no longer. It was by now receiving plenty of 5·9s and was rapidly losing the character of the quiet, well-to-do little town in which part of the Division was to have been billeted when it left the Amiens district. Still, for the time being, what St. Venant received in shells it paid for in choice vintages and fine houses. The Germans were not the only people to taste a glass of French wine during the Great War. About this time Colonel Boyle, who had commanded the 6th Oxfords until their disbandment, arrived to assume command of the Battalion. He remained till Wetherall, whose wound had taken him to England, returned.

For the rest of April and during May the Battalion continued to do tours in the Robecq sector, which, owing to its proximity to Givenchy and Béthune, was never quiet so long as the enemy was planning to attack those places. An alteration of the front was brought about on April 23, when the Gloucesters under Colonel Lawson advanced in co-operation with the 4th Division and captured Riez du Vintage and La Pierre au Beurre. Of this victory some spoils fell to the Battalion, which was holding the front line. Company Sergeant-Major Moss, of D Company, who went out to reconnoitre two hours after the attack had taken place, brought in forty-five prisoners, and during the following night half-a-dozen machine-guns were collected by the company.

German shelling at this time was often heavy. The tracks across the open up to the front line were rendered specially unpleasant by the pernicious '106' fuzes, with which the enemy's artillery was well supplied. From Robecq, which was steadily being shelled to ruins and through which one passed with reluctance, a disinterested salvage party, consisting of Stanley and the officers of B Company, brought a piano, which was destined to be an historic instrument. On more than one occasion the Battalion returned from its spell in the front line to the St. Venant Asylum, a large institution said to be the second largest of the kind in France. Its protesting inmates had been removed in lorries at the time of the German capture of Merville, and the long galleries and rooms thereafter became filled with troops. The ample bath-house, laundry, and kitchen of the Asylum, though ravaged by shelling and rifled by the mysterious depredations of looters, more than provided for the Battalion's wants. I have to record a very regrettable incident in connection with St. Venant Asylum. On the morning of May 21, during some shelling, when most of us had descended to cover, a German shell pierced the building where C and D Company Headquarters were and dropped through into the cellar, where it exploded. Several men were killed and also 'Tommy' Lodge, the officer whose conduct had earned him distinction three weeks before at Baquerolle Farm. Robinson, too, was wounded and was lost to the Battalion.

At the Asylum, despite its comfort, it was difficult to feel at ease. On May 7 the Orderly Room was struck full on its door by a 5·9. Headquarters had many an anxious moment (as when a large aeroplane bomb was heard coming through the air; it fell 30 yards from the Mess). At the end of May rest billets were altered to La Pierrière, a small straggling village west of the La Bassée Canal, where few shells fell but whither the civilians were as yet timid to return. At La Pierrière, whenever the Battalion came out for its four days' rest, the Canteen was established on the most up-to-date lines with a full stock, including beer and the current newspapers from England. During the summer several local papers were kind enough to send me copies every week for free distribution to the men. I make this an opportunity to thank Mr. Stanley Wilkins and the Bucks Comforts Fund for most generous gifts of 'smokes,' which more than once helped to stave off a cigarette famine.

The Canteen, though I have not before mentioned it, was a great feature in Battalion life. For the last eight months of the war, while I was President of the Regimental Institute, I was most anxious that our Canteen should be as good as possible. But my anxiety would have been worthless without the industry and enthusiasm of Lance-Corporal Kaye and Private Warburton, who managed every detail.

At this stage in my history, when, almost reluctantly, I am drawing towards its close, there are many features of the Battalion life which crowd upon me in their demand for mention. The Pioneers lining out for their match in six-a-side football against the Shoemakers and Tailors, the Stores piled high with 'hay-packs' and wicker baskets filled with unissued signalling equipment, Sergeant Birt quietly demanding last month's war-diary, Connell the arch-footballer, Kettle, the Sergeant-Cook, arguing about an oven, and the four Company Quartermaster-Sergeants whose vote was always unanimous—to proceed further would be to enumerate a list of people and things over whom it is my regret to pass so rapidly.

At the end of my chapters I have so often shown the Battalion marching back to rest that I shall leave it this time in the line. You must picture a medley of small fields and orchards, bounded on one side by the Calonne-Robecq road (which is the avenue of supply to the front line and much shelled) and on the other by the small streams called Noc and Clarence. Among the orchards stand numerous farmsteads, of which a large one known as Gloucester Farm had been our Battalion Headquarters in 1916, during a period of back-area rest. It has again been Battalion Headquarters. Recently the farm was shelled and the Berks Colonel, then in occupation, quitted it in favour of a two-storied house called Carvin. In the domed cellar of Baquerolle Farm—an old-fashioned building looking out across a wide midden to numerous cowsheds and outhouses—were usually the headquarters of C or D Companies and the Trench-Mortars. This farm was freely shelled. On April 24 the early-morning attention of the German guns set fire to the buildings; and Robinson was obliged to leave the cellar and repair with his headquarters to a trench to windward. The Posts themselves, as spring deepened into summer, became half lost in the crops and grass, until many of them could be reached in daylight. This fact, combined with his undaunted spirit of enterprise, led Colonel Lawson of the Gloucesters to crawl forward one morning to the German lines. His reckless bravery paid the penalty, for he was killed when only a short way from where a German post was lurking. Lawson was a brilliant soldier and a fine example of English character; his sudden and needless death cast a gloom over the whole Brigade.

On the evening of May 13 the last raid to be made by the Battalion was carried out by No. 13 Platoon, commanded by Rowlerson. The affair was a small one but satisfactory, for two prisoners were brought in and we had no casualties.

Chapter XVI.

THE TURNING OF THE TIDE,

May, June, July, August, 1918.

Rations and the Battalion Transport.—At La Lacque.—The bombing of Aire.—General Mackenzie obliged by his wound to leave the Division.—Return of Colonel Wetherall.—Tripp's Farm on fire.—A mysterious epidemic.—A period of wandering.—The march from Pont Asquin to St. Hilaire.—Nieppe Forest.—Attack by A and B Companies on August 7.—Headquarters gassed.—A new Colonel.—The Battalion goes a-reaping.

THOUGH used to being told that our army was the best fed of any in the war, few English people have any idea how rations reached the line. They came up every day from the Base by train as far as Railhead—which meant a convenient station as far forward as possible while still being outside the range of ordinary German guns—and were thence conveyed, normally in lorries, by the A.S.C. to the various 'refilling points' assigned to Infantry Brigades. From the refilling point, which was only a stretch of the roadside, the Transport collected the Battalion's rations and delivered them to the Quartermaster's stores; and by means of the Transport the Quartermaster, after their necessary division between companies, fowarded rations to the front line. Latterly it was rarely possible to cook in the trenches and it never was during active operations, so to Murray, our Quartermaster, and his staff fell the duty of sending up cooked food. It is impossible for me here to explain the system practised; but by means of food-containers, specially improvised from petrol tins and rammed into packs stuffed with hay, we were able to supply the men with hot food in the front line. Murray's organisation was excellent, and the four Company Quartermaster-Sergeants—Holder, Freudemacher, Taylor, and Beechey—and the Company Cooks earned equal credit in the performance of these important duties, which never miscarried.

The Battalion was fortunate in keeping as its Transport officer 'Bob' Abraham. He suited the job, and the job him. He had organised the Transport in 1914 and brought it overseas. Several pairs of mules, which had come out with the Battalion in 1916, were still at work and thriving three years later. By a riding accident Abraham was lost to the Battalion for a time, but his place was taken by Kirk, who proved himself an excellent substitute, and when Kirk left Woodford carried on with equal efficiency.

Long before the war was reaching its close I had ceased really to envy the Transport Officer, nor did our men in the trenches forget the responsibilities and danger of the drivers. In their turn the transport men felt that it was their duty to make up for the part they were not called upon to play with bomb and bayonet by never failing to deliver promptly and faithfully at company headquarters their limber-loads of rations. In its turn-out, whether at a Brigade horse-show, a veterinary inspection, or on the line of march, our Transport set a high standard; men and animals were alike a credit to the Battalion.

During the warm weather of the spring, when the canal banks were lined with bathers, our Transport was situated at La Lacque, a village a few miles west of Aire. Not far off stood the tall chimneys of the Isbergues steel works—a large factory, which, like Cassel and Dunkirk, had in the early days of the war attracted occasional shells from German long-range guns. Now that the line was only a few leagues distant the steel works became the almost daily target for 'high velocities.' Once the tiles had been shaken from the workshops no visible damage seemed to result from the many hundred shells which fell inside the factory's area. None the less the continuous shifts of workmen afforded a striking example of the national devotion of French industry, to be compared with that total dislocation of London business which even an air-raid warning was sufficient to engender. Isbergues village was now crowded with Portuguese, who spent their time tormenting dogs and washing themselves in the canal, but who officially were employed in making trenches, which they could be trusted to dig deep. At La Lacque a second Brigade School was established. The details of its management were under Coombes, who possessed considerable ability in this direction. The Battalion instructors were Sergeants Brooks and Brazier, both of whom were well versed in regimental drill and tradition and shewed much zeal in the work. Than Sergeant

Brazier no more hearty sportsman ever belonged to the Battalion.

At the end of May, 1918, when the whereabouts of his next attack were yet uncertain, the enemy's power reached its apparent zenith. A Canadian corps had been in reserve along the line of the La Bassée Canal for three weeks in expectation of a renewed attempt against Hazebrouck and Béthune. From prisoners' statements more than once an attack upon the Battalion seemed imminent and special precautions were adopted. All this time our artillery had been recovering its ascendancy, until the enemy, cooped up as he was within a salient bounded by canals, became faced with the two alternatives of attack or retreat. Meanwhile his aircraft used the fine nights of the early summer to wreak the utmost spite on our back area. During one night Aire, which had hitherto been left unscathed, was so severely bombed that one could have fancied the next day that the town had been convulsed by an earthquake. St. Omer, though less damaged, was frequently attacked. In northern France the visits of German aeroplanes became such that all towns, alike by military and civil populations, came to be deserted before nightfall.

How I should introduce appropriately and with becoming respect a reference to our Major-General has somewhat puzzled me. Sir Colin Mackenzie, K.C.B., had commanded the 61st Division through many difficult vicissitudes. His watchful eye and quiet manner gained everywhere the confidence and admiration of his regimental subordinates, who saw in him great soldierly qualities. The General's bearing and his string of real war-ribbons made many an eye rove at an inspection. By a wound he was obliged in June, 1918, to retire from command of the Division. He was much missed.

Towards the end of May Colonel Wetherall returned to take command of the Battalion. To be his Second in Command was both a pleasure and a privilege. Similar feelings were evoked towards the Brigadier, General Pagan, in whose small frame beat a lion's heart. When the frontage of the Brigade was changed from one to two battalions, we had to give up Baquerolle and Carvin and occupy instead the barren fields on the other side of the Calonne road, where most wretched front-line accommodation existed. Headquarters for the new sector were in Les Amusoires; and rations came up each night as far as a farm, called Tripp's Farm, forward of which neither cooking could be done nor any water obtained. One night German shelling, that tune to which rations were usually carried, set light to Tripp's Farm. Quartermaster-Sergeants, mules' heads, and guides were mingled in the glare, while from a concrete pill-box hard by machine-gunners (its rightful occupants) were compelled to avoid roasting by flight. About this time both St. Venant and Robecq were burning for several days. Of the former, most of the remaining houses near the church (which had been frequently struck) were destroyed, but in Robecq the fire almost confined itself to the famous café near the cross-roads. To quench these conflagrations no measures were, or could be, taken, for their occurrence was a great gratification to the German artillery, which always redoubled its efforts in the hope of spreading a fire as far as possible.

In the middle of June, during a stay at La Pierrière, the Battalion was ravaged by a mysterious epidemic, which claimed hundreds of victims before it passed. Starting among the signallers, it first spread through Headquarters, and then attacked all Companies indiscriminately. Among the officers, Cubbage and Shields (the doctor) were the first to go to hospital; soon followed by Clutsom, who was adjutant at this time, and Tobias, the very doctor who had come to replace Shields. The Colonel and myself were the next victims, and when the time came for the Battalion to go into the line, it was necessary to send for Christie-Miller, of the Gloucesters, to take command and to make Murray from quartermaster into adjutant. This epidemic was not confined to the Battalion, nor to the 61st Division. Isolation camps had hastily to be formed, for the evil threatened to dislocate whole corps and even armies. Among the Germans the same complaint seems to have spread with even greater virulence; indeed, it may well have prevented them from launching a further offensive against Béthune and Hazebrouck. By doctors it was classified under the name of Pyrexia of Unknown Origin ('P.U.O.') while in such guarded references as occurred our Press spoke of it as 'Spanish Influenza.' The symptoms of the illness consisted in high temperature, followed by great physical and mental lassitude. Most cases recovered within a week, but some took longer, nor was a second attack following recovery from the first at all uncommon. Such was the only epidemic of the war. Thanks to the care and efficiency of our Regimental M.O.s the dreaded scourges of past wars—cholera, dysentery, and enteric—in France could together claim few, if any, victims.

On June 25 it was time for the 184th Infantry Brigade to move out of the line to Ham and Linghem, two villages south-east and south of Aire. The relief took place, but at the last minute it was decided that the 182nd Brigade was so depleted by the epidemic that it was necessary for the 2/4th Oxfords to remain at La Pierrière to assist them in holding the line. At the Brigade sports, held at Linghem on July 7, the Battalion easily carried off the cup offered for competition by General Pagan. In the relay race Sergeant Brazier accomplished a fine performance, while in the boxing we showed such superiority that no future Brigade competition ever took place.[1]

Before we left La Pierrière what can well be looked back to as a red-letter day was spent in sports and a full programme of entertainments, including the Divisional 'Frolics,' who were prevailed on to perform in a farmyard. Jimmy Kirk also brought his coaching party of clowns—who on this occasion avoided a conflict with the Military Police—and of course the Battalion Band regaled us with choice items throughout the day. In the sports a race had to be re-run because one of the competitors, instead of waiting for the 'pistol'

[1] In the realm of sport a later achievement of the Battalion deserves record. On July 27 at the XI Corps horse-show our team won the open tug-of-war.

THE HEADQUARTERS RUNNERS, JULY 1918.

THE TURNING OF THE TIDE, 1918.

(A. E. G. Bennett with home-made 'blanks') started at the report of our 6-inch gun in the next orchard, which occurred a fraction of a second earlier. The evening was saved from bathos by the news that the Division was to be relieved. Life operates by contrast, and though the war was going on a few miles to the eastward I believe as much pleasure was experienced that day in the small orchard behind Headquarters at La Pierrière as in any elaborate peace celebration in this country. Indeed, to see the crowd 'celebrating' the armistice up and down the Strand was enough to make one recall with regret such an occasion of the war as I have described.

On July 10 we moved back, most of the way by 'bus, to Liettres, a very pretty village well behind the line and south-west of Aire. Hardly were we settled before we were ordered to move, which we did with no very good grace to St. Hilaire, a much inferior village. Two days later our tactical location was discovered to be still unsatisfactory, so we tried a march northwards to Warne, where for the third time in ten days a quartermaster's store had to be built from the materials we had managed to drag along with us. Almost before our headquarter runners had learnt the whereabouts of companies we were on the road again. This time we left the XI Corps, with which so many of the Battalion's fortunes and misfortunes had been associated, and passed into General Plumer's Army as part of the XV Corps. The paradise which every division, sent back for 'rest,' fancies will have been prepared for it, now degenerated to a mere field. Still, there are many worse places, if some better, than a grass field; footballs were soon bouncing merrily, and on the air floated the monotonous enumeration of 'House.' One evening the Colonel, myself, and the company commanders returned wet-through from a voyage of inspection of the Hazebrouck defences, for a German attack was still anticipated. The last of these shuttle-cock moves occurred on July 31, from our field at Pont Asquin back to St. Hilaire, whose billets few of us were anxious to revisit.

As I have not loaded my narrative with marches my readers shall hoist full pack (no air-pillows allowed!) upon their backs and fall in with the Battalion. It is already dusk as the sanitary men, like so many sorcerers, stoop in the final rites of fire and burial. Some days ago I taxed the bandmaster, Bond, with the possibility of playing in the dark; for a moment his face was as long as Taylor's bassoon, but since then by means of surreptitious practice and, I fancy, the sheer confiscation of his bandsmen's folios, the impossible has been achieved. Every band is the best in France, but only ours can play in darkness. Thus, as the column swings past the pond and waiting cookers, the Band strikes up one of its best and loudest marches. . . .

Such midnight music, if it drowned the drone of German aeroplanes, which ever and anon swam overhead, looking like white moths in the beams of our searchlights, served also to arouse the village inhabitants, whose angry faces were framed for an instant in windows as we passed. Our musical uproar set dogs barking for miles, cocks crowed at our passage, and generals turned in their second sleep to hear such martial progress in the night. The march—through Racquinghem and Aire—was long, lasting nearly all night. To flatter its interest a sweepstake had been arranged among the officers for who should name the exact moment of its conclusion. Years of foot-slogging in France made my considered guess formidable in the competition. More dangerous still was that of the Colonel, for to him would fall the duty of the decisive whistle-blast, and his entry ultimately was not accepted by the 'committee.' As in most sweepstakes, the first prize fell to a most undeserving winner.

July closed with a feeling of dissatisfaction at the cycle of moves which had rendered futile both rest and training. Consciousness that one was helping to win the war was more often imputed than felt. Early in August, 1918, the 61st relieved the 5th Division in front of the Nieppe Forest. Minor attacks had already cleared the enemy from the eastern fringe of the forest and driven him back towards Neuf Berquin and Merville. At 7 p.m. on August 7 A and B Companies attacked and captured the trenches opposite to them, causing the enemy to retire behind the Plate Becque, a stream as wide as the Cherwell at Islip but far less attractive. We had a dozen casualties in this attack, which was rewarded by half as many German prisoners and a machine-gun. Sergeant Ravenscroft, of B Company, for an able exploit during the advance, received the D.C.M.

Already the Forest of Nieppe had become notorious for German gas. It was now a nightly

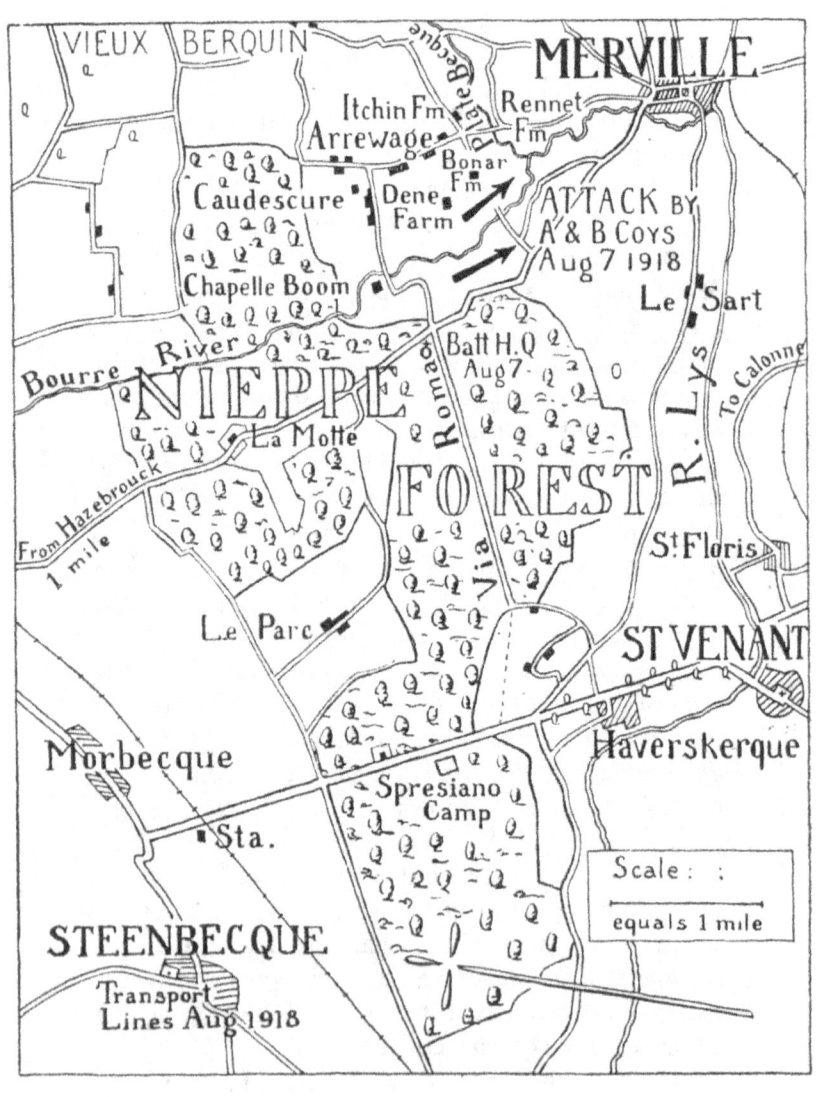

programme of the enemy to drench the wood, which was low-lying and infested with pools and undergrowth, with his noxious 'Yellow Cross'—shells whose poisonous fumes bore the flavour of mustard. Throughout the night of August 7/8, when things generally were very active, a heavy gas-bombardment was kept up. The Colonel was away from his headquarters at the time. He returned after the shelling to find that gas helmets had been taken off. No harm was expected, but the next day, after the sun's heat had awakened dormant fumes, the Colonel, Symonds (the adjutant), Kirk, who had brought up the rations, and Cubbage, as well as the Regimental Sergeant-Major and many signallers and runners, all found that they were gassed. Their loss was serious. It was known that Wetherall would soon have to leave the Battalion, for he had been appointed to a command in the Machine Gun Corps; indeed already his successor, Colonel Woulfe-Flanagan, had arrived to take his place. Under the present unlucky auspices (for more than half Headquarters were knocked out) the interchange took place.

Herodotus says of the kings of Sparta that the last was always regretted as the best the country had ever had. Colonel Wetherall's merit did not depend on his being the last of a series. Phrases such as 'he was worshipped by the men' have become so hackneyed as to be meaningless, nor shall I use an even worse commonplace, that 'he was sparing of his words.' Wetherall was just a rattling good Commanding Officer, a true friend, and a fine soldier. His successor, E. M. Woulfe-

Flanagan, came from the East Surreys. He bore a distinguished record of pre-war service and had been wounded in the Mons retreat. A regular soldier of the old school, in ideas and methods he differed widely from his predecessor. But he was worth his salt every time. Certainly no braver officer ever set foot in France.

After we had finished our first tour in the Nieppe Forest sector, both the Berks and Gloucesters were sent forward against the enemy, who was rightly suspected by the staff to be on the point of retreating from the Lys salient. The attack had to cross the Plate Becque, whose eastern bank the enemy was fighting hard to hold. Gloucesters and Berks rushed forward at misty dawn and flung bridges over the stream; but the machine-gun fire was too intense, and though some parties got across, others did not, co-operation broke down, and the attack gained no result. A few days afterwards the Germans went back, giving up Calonne, Merville, and Neuf Berquin—villages which our artillery had utterly pulverised. As in the March retreat of 1917, the 184th Brigade had no immediate share in following up the enemy as he retired. The Oxfords had withdrawn on August 14 to Spresiano Camp, in the forest, and waited without eagerness to be ordered forward to the new devastated area. It is curious to reflect that at this time, so distant did the end of the war still seem, we grumbled at losing our comfortable base at Steenbecque, which we hoped to keep perhaps through the winter. Most thinking people could see neither value nor wisdom in pursuing the Germans in their retreats, planned

and carried out in their own time, from salients. Hardly on one occasion did we hustle them, and the policy, deprecated by most commanders of lower formations, of snatching at the first morsels of abandoned territory always cost us heavy casualties. Between war and chess there is a close analogy. In front of Nieppe Forest there were now a hopeless crowding of the pieces, moves aimlessly made from square to square, and the reckless calling of 'check,' which to a good opponent means time and renewed chances to escape defeat.

During the early stages of the retreat the Battalion was sent to fresh fields of conquest among the crops, which the German withdrawal had done nothing to ripen but had at least removed from shell range. Plans were afoot to harvest a large area adjacent to the forest and present its fruits to the rightful owners. If harvesting weather should be hot, conditions were ideal. This novel form of working-party at first delighted the men, who set about the crops in goodly earnest. In a short space of time wheat, oats, and barley were added to our battle-honours. But if the spirit was willing, our reaping implements were correspondingly weak. The Corps 'Agricultural Officer' had collected from surrounding farms a fantastic assortment of cast-off scythes, jagged hooks, and rusty sickles, which fell to pieces 'in the 'ands' and refused to do more than beat down the crops to which they were opposed. The scythes seemed hardly able to stick their points, in the approved manner, into the ground, sickles were back-to-front or left-handed, and the entire panoply issued to this Reaping Battalion should have been seconded for duty at a music-hall or gazetted out of agricultural service as old iron. The Major-General, visiting the scene of our labours, was scandalised to find that fewer acres of corn had been put out of action than reports from other parts of the harvest front inclined him to expect. A 'stinker' followed, to which we could only retaliate by posting sentries the next day to warn us of the General's approach. Of course he came by a fresh road. And now, to avoid the inevitable anti-climax, I will ring down the curtain as the General steps from his car, demoralised reapers bestir themselves into some semblance of activity, and the commander of the party simply is not.

Chapter XVII.

LAST BATTLES,

August to December, 1918.

German retreat from the Lys.—Orderly Room and its staff.—The new devastated area.—Itchin Farm, Merville and Neuf Berquin.—Mines and booby-traps.—Advance to the Lys.—Estaires destroyed.—Laventie revisited.—The attack on Junction Post.—Lance-Corporal Wilcox, V.C.—Scavenging at the XI Corps school.—On the Aubers ridge.—The end in sight.—Move to Cambrai.—In action near Bermerain and Maresches.—A fine success.—Domart and Demobilisation.—Work at Etaples.—Off to Egypt.

WHILE the Battalion harvested the corn behind Nieppe Forest, on the other side of it hue and cry were being raised after the enemy, whose tail was well turned in his last retreat. The Lys salient, which had proved so useless to him, was being evacuated. On the evening of August 20, 1918, the Battalion was ordered forward from Spresiano Camp to occupy the old trenches near Chapelle Boom, a quaint moated farmhouse on the eastern outskirts of the forest. We found the area already overstocked with troops; indeed Chapelle Boom itself, though assigned to us, was the headquarters of not less than two units of the 183rd Infantry Brigade. The arrival of the Battalion, loaded as it was with the encumbrances of advance, further contributed to the congestion. In a few days the Suffolks and Northumberland Fusiliers suddenly disappeared, and Chapelle Boom fell into our power. There we stayed until the Colonel went upon a course.

As usually when the Germans genuinely retired, to use their own phrase, 'according to plan,' early

immunity from shells preluded days when the last spite of their artillery was flung as far as possible. Harassing fire against our exits from Nieppe Forest was cleverly manipulated by the enemy. Our guns, which had the choice of few orchards or buildings to screen their flashes, were vigorously searched for when they opened fire. Bonar Farm, Dene Farm, Rennet Farm—places of ill name during the fighting for the Plate Becque—were freely shelled. From the explosion of a chance 4.2 Ellis and several men in D Company were casualties. Whilst in reserve we bathed in the river and for a time resumed our harvesting pursuits. The method became more unique and amateur than ever—we were directed to pluck the ripe ears of corn by hand. I laid down the standard task of one sandbag-full per day per man. Some men used nail-scissors, and it was found that a 'one hour day' was ample to ensure a good 'return.' Soon a pile of bags lay by the roadside. One wonders instinctively what became of the corn and whether it was used.

The word 'return' should set some readers agog. I am sure no battalion had a better Orderly Room than the 2/4th Oxfords. Though only a Company Commander, I was struck by its efficiency when I joined the Battalion. Units were apt to be judged by the promptness and accuracy of their returns, and Cuthbert, who for longer than anyone was Adjutant of the Battalion, won a deserved reputation in this respect. But inside the Battalion as well as out of it his efficiency was understood and valued. Cuthbert was a good instance of an officer without pre-war training whose common-sense and agreeability made him the equal in his work of any Regular. In the office Sergeant Birt had now for two years been a pillar of reliability; few officers or men of the Battalion but owed something to him. Spring 1918 brought an interregnum in the adjutantcy, till R. F. Symonds, formerly of the Bucks, returned from a staff attachment to take the post. Symonds had a remarkable gift for office work.

Wrapped up in the routine of the Battalion, he was never happier than in Orderly Room with a full 'basket.' Since the gassing of Headquarters, Shilson, a recently arrived officer with antecedents in the A.S.C., had acted adjutant; right creditably did he acquit himself in the duties suddenly cast upon him. Other new officers were now filling important positions in the Battalion. Faithfull, another disciple from the A.S.C., whom also we got to like very much, was now in command of D Company; Clutsom commanded C, and Young, who had seen long service with the 48th Division, B Company; Jones still led A. Time had wrought changes among the Sergeant-Majors of the Companies. At this period in Cunningham of A, Mudd of B, Smith of C, and Brooks of D, we had a quartet of tried experience. The recurrent conflicts about 'strength'—a word which in effect meant the number of men employed with Quartermaster's Stores and at Headquarters—were now at a high pitch. After much 'camouflage,' by aid of Bicknell, of the real facts, we had reluctantly to choose between the 'return to duty' in the line of either Band or Buglers. The choice was hard, but in the end we kept the Band intact, for loss of a few bandsmen as casualties might leave such gaps as would prevent the Band from playing at all.

On August 24 we relieved the 5th Suffolks in the outpost line, which had remained stationary for several days. It lay upon the eastern fringe of Neuf Berquin, through whose scattered ruins one picked a way to find the posts. Headquarters were some distance back, but most wretchedly accommodated in an orchard close to a lonely brick-stack known as Itchin Farm. . The German guns showed marked persistency, not actually against the holes which formed Headquarters, but all around. No area more dismal could be imagined than the flat, dyke-ridden country north of Merville. So thoroughly had our artillery during the last four months plastered the ground behind his former lines that little scope had been left for the retreating frenzy of the enemy. By bombs and shells we had driven the Germans not only from such places as Merville and Neuf Berquin, but from the mere proximity to roads or houses. They had concealed themselves as best they could in ditches and narrow tunnels made with corrugated iron or planks. The 'Huns,' indeed, had been meeting with their deserts. Their life in the Lys salient must have been a nightmare. One required only to read a few of the notices displayed to realise the difference of life behind their line and ours. Everywhere appeared in big letters the word 'Fliegerdeckung!' *i.e.* cover from aircraft. No testimony more eloquent of British superiority could have been offered.

Further behind, round Estaires and La Gorgue, the Germans were busy blowing up and burning ere their retreat ebbed back across the Lys. Black palls of smoke rose daily from where mills and factories were aflame. One day the tall church of Sailly had simply vanished; the next, one looked vainly for Estaires' square tower. Often, when idly scanning the horizon or watching aeroplanes, eyes were arrested by huge jets which sprang into the air to become clouds as large as any in the sky.

Combining with this present orgy of destruction numerous booby-traps were left behind, whose action was delayed till our advance should provide victims for their murderous art. Cross-roads and level-crossings especially 'went up,' or were expected to, and so many houses were mined that it became impossible to rest secure in any. In fact, the 182nd Brigade ordered its men out of all buildings. Some measure of vile ingenuity must be accorded to the authors of these booby-traps; but whether bombs under beds or attached to pump handles can be included in legitimate warfare is a case for judgment.

At short notice we attacked from Neuf Berquin on August 28. In some places the advance was quite successful, but in others not. German counter-attacks obliged A Company, which had made good progress south of the Neuf Berquin—Estaires road in the morning, to withdraw its patrols at dusk. A few days later, however, the opposition lessened, and companies went forward several miles. Soon afterwards the 182nd Brigade took turn as the advanced guard, the Lys was reached and crossed, and presently patrols were passing through the old 'posts' and grass-grown breastworks which used to lie behind our front-line system. We followed, and for several days lived in reserve among the scattered farms and houses north of Estaires, over the ruins of which Crosthwaite, an officer of mature service, who had just joined the Battalion, was appointed Town Major. His task was not entirely enviable. Houses, roofless or otherwise, had to be subdivided into safe, doubtful, or certain to 'go up.' I cannot help regarding this Flanders retreat as a subject supremely dull. The constant suspicion of mines and booby-traps rendered doubly sordid the polluted ruins which formed the landmarks of our advance. One feature alone provided interest to some. We were approaching, from an odd direction as it seemed, the old area where the Battalion had first held its trenches. La Gorgue, Estaires, Laventie were places rich in association. How much the two former were altered! La Gorgue, where in 1916 Divisional Headquarters and Railhead had been, was heaped in ugly ruin. Its expensive church had been blown in two. Of Estaires proper little more than its charred walls remained. In such shape was victory passing into our hands.

When the enemy was holding the line Picantin—Junction Post, the Battalion went forward to hold an outpost line north-east of Laventie. On September 10, while he was taking over his new piece of front, Clutsom, of C Company, was badly wounded by a German shell. No officer could have been more regretted. I am glad to say his wound healed steadily and he was soon writing cheerful letters to his friends from England. Command of his company passed to Stanley.

Headquarters now were in the old dressing station at Laventie. It was a house of quite pretentious size, left standing by the enemy. Although its floors were heaped with shavings, prophets of all ranks assigned a violent end to tenants of such a residence. For the next tour we

CORPORAL A. WILCOX, V.C.

were content to move into Laventie North Post, but all the time the house belied our fears, nor have I evidence that any mine existed. I walked through the village, and I must say it seemed less damaged than I had expected. Most of its buildings were quite recognisable. The house formerly Battalion Headquarters might, with labour, have been made to serve again. The line of small plane trees, which gave Laventie the meretricious semblance of a garden city, was standing yet. In the war's passage over it Laventie suffered less havoc than had seemed probable.

At a few hours' notice and in weather calculated to make any operation a fiasco, the Battalion on September 12 attacked Junction Post, a grass-bound breastwork where the enemy was offering a stubborn resistance. Though finally unsuccessful in result, the fighting, which was accompanied by driving storms of rain, produced two noteworthy incidents. Rowlerson, one of C Company's platoon commanders, after reaching the German trenches, somehow lost touch and was captured with several of his men. In A Company an exploit was performed, which gained for the Battalion its second Victoria Cross. Lance-Corporal Wilcox came to close quarters with some enemy defending a piece of trench with four machine-guns. Each of these guns Lance-Corporal Wilcox, followed by his section, successively captured or put out of action. Wilcox was shortly afterwards wounded and was in hospital in England when news of the award arrived. His deed lent lustre to a profitless attack.

A few days later the Battalion was relieved and spent a period in reserve among fields and orchards west of Sailly-sur-la-Lys. We suffered much from the night-long attention of the German 'pip-squeak' guns, whose range, longer considerably than that of the English 18-pounder, was made fullest use of by the enemy. A move came as a welcome surprise. Under mysterious directions the Battalion was ordered back as far as Linghem, a village I have mentioned before as lying south of Aire. Arrived there, we were placed in some huts, destined for eventual occupation by the XI Corps school. More than a day elapsed before the object of our visit was explained: the Battalion was to sweep and clean the camp for its inspection by the Corps Commander. We were not present at the ceremony, but for a week preceding it all four companies were daily engaged weeding potato patches, tarring roofs, and evacuating a dump of several hundred thousand empty tins. Rarely were the energies of an Infantry Battalion more curiously devoted.

At Laventie no startling events had filled our absence. But after our return—Junction Post had not yet fallen, so that the outpost line was still in front of Rouge de Bout—developments began. On September 30 the enemy lost Junction Post to a spirited attack by the Gloucesters, the line that he had been holding for three weeks was broken, and his retreat became fast and general. After relieving the Gloucesters our companies were hard put to it to advance rapidly enough to keep touch. At last we stood upon the Aubers Ridge itself. Lille was

LAST BATTLES, AUGUST—DECEMBER, 1918.

almost in view; but at this point the Division was relieved by the 59th and sent southwards to join our armies before Cambrai, where the final issue between British and German arms was destined to be decided.

Out of the closing phases of the war I feel there must be material from which historians will find that climax which so grand a conflict deserves as its termination. But I confess that I find scarcely any.

After its dramatic and sinister opening the war seemed almost belittled by its tame conclusion. Years of nerve-racking experiences, the hardships, and the immutable association which towns like Ypres, Arras and Albert, and the trench-dwellings of Flanders and the Somme possessed, had indisposed the mind to receive new impressions from the last battle of the war. Patient from a hundred moves from trench to billet, from billet to trench, the British soldier accepted with characteristic resignation moves which were sweeping him to Victory. By gas, liquid fire, night-flying aeroplanes, and long-range artillery, the war had in four years demonstrated the incredible. The mere collapse, on one side, of the agencies military and political which lay behind, was in itself commonplace.

The Battalion joined the XVII Corps half way through October, 1918, and was soon put into important fighting. The enemy, who had lost Lille, Douai, and St. Quentin early in the month, was now in full retreat between Verdun and the sea. To preserve his centre from being pierced and his flanks rolled up, rearguards eastward of Cambrai were offering the maximum resistance. Most villages, though they passed into our hands nearly intact and in some cases full of civilians, had to be fought for. The German machine-gunners rarely belied their character of fighting to the end. In an attack on October 24 from Haussy, the Battalion, advancing rapidly in artillery formation, captured the high ground east of Bermerain; and the next day B and D Companies (the latter now commanded by Cupper) again attacked, and captured the railway south-east of Sepmeries. For these operations the weather was fine, the ground dry, and the leadership excellent. A period followed in reserve at Vendegies and afterwards at Bermerain, villages which were liberally bombarded by the German long-range guns. Moving up again on November 2, the Battalion made its last attack of the war. A fine success resulted. The objectives—St. Hubert and the ridge east of it—were captured, together with 700 prisoners, 40 machine-guns, and 4 tanks, recently used by the enemy in a counter-attack. The fruits of this victory were well deserved by the Battalion, the more because so often in the course of the war it had been set to fight against odds in secondary operations. It was a good wind-up.

Of some battalions it was said that on November 11, 1918 they found themselves standing within a mile or two of where they first went into action in 1914. We, naturally, could claim no such coincidence; yet a dramatic touch was not wanting when the telegram, which bore the news of the cessation of hostilities, was read out by the Colonel to a

OFFICERS OF THE BATTALION, DECEMBER 1918.

GENERAL THORNE AND 184TH INFANTRY BRIGADE STAFF, CHRISTMAS 1918.

LAST BATTLES, AUGUST—DECEMBER, 1918.

parade formed up at Maresches upon the very ground whence the Battalion had started in its last attack.

The Battalion was never in the Army on the Rhine. After time spent at Cambrai we travelled back to Domart, a village mid-way between Amiens and Abbeville. In duration the journey surpassed all records. Three days we spent impatiently waiting for a train, and two more patiently waiting in the train itself; and we arrived at the destination faced with a ten-mile march in rain and pitch darkness. Happily the war was still sufficiently recent for such delay to pass as comedy. At Domart the one real topic was Demobilisation. I could set myself no harder task than a description of the workings of this engine. Few people understood how they were themselves demobilised, and fewer cared how others were. That the scheme worked on the whole well and justly was in great measure due to Symonds, whose zealous energy, though the Battalion was lessoning daily, never flagged. For two months Battalion drill and the 'Education Scheme' occupied our mornings, football our afternoons. Christmas was a great festival. The 'Frolics' pantomime visited the village, in which the Battalion pioneers, under the direction of Cameron, the Brigade signalling officer, had transformed an empty building into a capital theatre. General Thorne, who had so successfully commanded the 184th Infantry Brigade in its last battle, was unstinting in his efforts to give the men's life in the army a happy and useful conclusion. He secured visits from all the best concert parties and raised a fund to finance the department of Brigade entertainments, of which Nicholas, the Brigade Major, was chief minister. A weekly magazine was started, which ran to its fourth number. Truly the arts flourished.

In a windy field south of the village the Battalion was in January presented with its colour by Major-General Duncan. The occasion passed off well. Its feature was the admirable speech made by the Colonel.

In February the Battalion, which it was known would be made up with drafts and retained for service as a unit, was sent to Etaples to assist in the Demobilisation scheme. For a month we remained meeting trains, escorting parties to camps, sorting clothing, and driving herds of the demobilised through the intricacies of a machine called the 'Delouser,' until the arriving trainloads decreased, dwindled, and finally stopped. In March several large drafts of officers and men, to replace all those who had been, or would be, demobilised, joined the Battalion, which, after a pause at Le Tréport and some leave, sailed for Egypt. Thither my story does not follow it. When peace was signed, the cadre of the Battalion had not returned to Oxford. On Christmas Day 1919 the 2/4th Oxfordshire and Buckinghamshire Light Infantry was still serving overseas.

THE ADJUTANT AT HIS DESK.

CAMBRAI: THE HOTEL DE VILLE.

THE BATTALION COOKS AT ETAPLES.

LIEUT.-COL. E. M. WOULFE-
FLANAGAN, C.M.G., D.S.O.

REGIMENTAL SERGT.-MAJOR
HEDLEY.

REGIMENTAL QUARTERMASTER-
SERGEANT HEDGES.

Composition of the Battalion on going overseas

Headquarters.

Colonel W. H. AMES, T.D.
Major G. P. R. BEAMAN, 2nd in Command.
Major D. M. ROSE, Adjutant.
Lieut. C. S. W. MARCON, Signalling Officer.
2/Lieut. H. E. COOMBES, Intelligence Officer.
Lieut. G. H. G. SHEPHERD, Machine-gun Officer.
Lieut. R. L. ABRAHAM, Transport Officer.
Lieut. W. A. HOBBS, Quartermaster.
Captain A. WORSLEY, Medical Officer.

Company Commanders.

Captain H. J. BENNETT, A Company.
Captain H. N. DAVENPORT, B Company.
Captain A. H. BRUCKER, C Company.
Captain R. F. CUTHBERT, D Company.

Regimental Sergeant-Major.

T. V. WOOD.

Regimental Quartermaster-Sergeant.

W. C. HEDGES.

Company Sergeant-Majors.

C. A. WITNEY, A Company.
A. BALL, B Company.
W. F. CAMPION, C Company.
W. DOUGLAS, D Company.

Composition of the Battalion at the Armistice

Headquarters.

Lieut.-Colonel E. M. WOULFE-FLANAGAN, C.M.G., D.S.O.
Major G. K. ROSE, M.C., 2nd in Command.
Captain R. F. SYMONDS, Adjutant.
Lieut. T. S. R. BOASE, M.C., Signalling Officer.
Lieut. W. A. F. HEARNE, Intelligence Officer.
Captain J. W. SHILSON, Assistant Adjutant.
Lieut. G. W. WOODFORD, M.C., Transport Officer.
Captain W. G. MURRAY, Quartermaster.
Lieut. E. P. NEARY (U.S.), Medical Officer.

Company Commanders.

Captain H. JONES, M.C., A Company.
Captain R. E. M. YOUNG, B Company.
Captain J. STANLEY, M.C., C Company.
Captain J. H. D. FAITHFULL, D Company.

Regimental Sergeant-Major.

W. HEDLEY, D.C.M.

Regimental Quartermaster-Sergeant.

W. C. HEDGES.

Company Sergeant-Majors.

C. R. HOLDER, A Company.
A. J. MUDD, B Company.
S. SMITH, D.C.M., C Company.
M. T. BROOKS, D Company.

INDEX

Ablaincourt, 55, 56, 75.
Abraham, Capt. R. L., 14, 80, 157, 172, 175, 193.
Aire, 194, 195, 201.
Aitken, Lieut. R., 85, 86.
Albert, 23.
Allden, Lieut. J. H., 84, 100, 101.
Ames, Col. W. H., 7, 13.
Amiens, 104, 174.
A.S.C., 43, 45, 132, 192.
Arras, 107, 111, 144.
Arrowsmith, Rev. W. L., M.C., 106.
Asylum, St. Venant, 188, 189.
Athies, 79.
Auxi-le-Château, 111, 112.
Aveluy, 35.
Avesne, 174-176.

Band, the, 200, 211.
Baquerolle Farm, 181, 183, 186, 189, 191, 196.
Barnes, Lance-Corpl., 109.
Barton, Lieut. C. J., 14, 86.
Bassett, Col.-Sgt., 1.
Baxter, Pte., 137, 139.
Beaman, Maj. G. P. R., 14, 66.
Beauvoir Line, 163-165.
Beechey, C.Q.-M.S., 193.
Bellamy, Lt.-Col. R., D.S.O., 14, 30, 43, 51, 104.
Bennett, Lieut. A. E. G., 199.
Bennett, Maj. H. J., M.C., 14, 15, 23, 43, 86, 92, 145, 164-170.
Berks, 2/4th Royal, 25, 35, 51, 55, 66, 77, 98, 102, 122, 124, 161, 163, 169, 170, 181, 204.
Bermerain, 218.
Bernaville, 111.
Bicknell, Capt. A., M.C., 34, 152, 211.
Birt, Sgt. J. W., 190, 210.
Boase, Lieut. T. S. R., M.C., 175, 182, 186.
Boyle, Lt.-Col. C. R. C., D.S.O., 187.
Brigade, 182nd Inf., 78, 85, 87, 160, 198, 213.
—— 183rd Inf., 126, 169, 208.

Brazier, Sgt., 194, 198.
Brooks, C.S.M. E., V.C., 34, 64, 66, 101, 117.
Brooks, Sgt. M. T., 194, 211.
Broomfield, 4.
Brown, Capt. K. E., M.C., 14, 23, 38, 40, 51, 56, 85, 117, 119, 132, 159, 171.
Broxeele, 114.
Brucamps, 49.
Brucker, Capt. A. H., 14, 117, 124.
Bucks, 2/1st, 35, 79, 81, 94, 125, 135, 158, 174, 175.
Buggins, Father, 79.
Buller, Sgt., 109.
Butcher, Sgt., M.M., 101.
Buttfield, Capt. L. F., M.C., 175, 182.

Cairns, C.S.M. J., D.C.M., 124, 125, 172.
Callender, Lieut. J. C., 14, 117, 119, 124.
Calonne, 177, 179-183, 204.
Calonne Road, 19, 183, 186, 190, 196.
Cambrai, 217, 219.
Cameron, Bde Signalling Officer, 219.
Canteen, the, 189, 190.
Carvin, 179, 191, 196.
Caulaincourt, 81, 86.
Cepy Farm, 94, 102, 160.
Chapelle Boom, 209.
Chaulnes, 49, 56, 60, 78, 79.
Chemical Works, 142, 149.
Chili Avenue, 143.
Chocques, 174, 177.
Christie-Miller, Lieut.-Col. G., D.S.O., M.C., 197.
Christmas Day, 41, 155, 219, 220.
Clarence River, 179, 191.
Clutsom, Capt. C. R., 175, 197, 211, 214.
Coles, Corpl., 63, 66.
Collett, Sgt., 30.
Connell, Bugler, 190.
Contay Wood, 22.

INDEX

Copinger, Lieut. J. P., 117, 140.
Coombes, Lieut. H. E., 117, 194.
Coucher, Lieut. G. W., 186.
Craddock, Lieut., 170.
Crosthwaite, Capt. H. T., 213.
Cubbage, Lieut., 197, 203.
Cunningham, C.S.M., 211.
Cunningham, Lieut. J. C., 159, 162.
Cupper, Lieut. H. J., 218.
Cuthbert, Capt. R. F., M.C., 14, 30, 51, 63, 149, 210.

Davenport, Capt. H. N., M.C., 7, 9, 14, 38, 75, 166, 168.
Davies, Pte. A. H., 137.
Dawson-Smith, Lieut. C. F., 117.
D.C.L.I., 1/5th, 34, 36, 166, 179.
Deniécourt, 51.
Desire Trench, 25, 26, 38.
Dimmer, Lt.-Col. J. S., V.C., 168.
Division, 4th, 185, 188.
,, 5th, 201.
,, 15th, 122, 126, 144.
,, 17th, 143.
,, 20th, 166, 168, 175.
,, 32nd, 55, 90.
,, 48th, 122, 124, 126.
,, 51st, 177, 179.
,, 59th, 84, 85, 217.
Domart, 219.
Douglas, R.S.M. W., 14, 172.
Doullens, 174, 177.
Dugan, Br.-Gen. W. J., C.M.G., D.S.O., 14.
Duncan, Maj.-Gen. F. J., C.B., C.M.G., D.S.O., 207, 220.

Ellis, Lieut., 210.
Enghien Redoubt, 160, 162, 165.
Estaires, 17, 212-214.
Etaples, 220.

Fabick Trench, 23.
Faithfull, Capt. J. H. D., 211.
Fauquissart, 10.
Fayet, 90, 94, 96, 98, 157, 158, 160-163, 171.
Field Trench, 36, 37.
Foreshew, Capt. C. E. P., M.C., 159.
Framerville, 76, 80.
Freudemacher, C.Q-M.S., 193.
'Frolics,' the, 198, 219.
Fry, Lieut., 61.

Gas, 114, 128, 136, 150, 203.
Gascoyne, Lieut., 117, 124.

Gepp, Bde.-Maj., 33, 148, 149.
Gloucester Farm, 19, 191.
Gloucesters, 2/5th, 15, 35, 84, 85, 90, 162, 163, 169, 170, 183, 184, 187, 188, 204, 216.
Goldfish Château, 120, 125-127.
Gonnelieu, 153, 154.
Goodman, Lance-Cpl., 140.
Gouzeaucourt, 152, 153.
Grandcourt, 24, 28.
Greenland Hill, 105, 149.
Guest, Lieut. H. R., M.C., 117, 125, 140.
Guildford, Lieut., 64.

Ham, 166, 168.
Hangest, 176.
Harbonnières, 49.
Harling, Major R. W., 34.
Harris, Capt. H. T. T., 117.
Hatt, Pte., D.C.M., 151.
Haussy, 218.
Havrincourt Wood, 154.
Hawkes, Lieut. T. W. P., 117.
Hazebrouck, 177, 195, 200.
Hedauville, 30, 33, 34, 43.
Hedges, R.Q-M.S. W. C., 14.
Hedley, R.S.M. W., D.C.M., 175, 203.
Herbert, Lieut. S. E., 109.
Hessian Trench, 30, 37, 38, 40.
Hill, Lieut. T. A., 117.
Hill 35, 131-140.
Hinton, Sgt., M.M, 15.
Hobbs, Capt. (Q.-M.) W. A., 14, 21, 45, 159.
Holder, C.Q-M.S. C. R., 193.
Holnon, 90, 91, 102, 157, 159, 162, 163.
Hombleux, 88, 166.
Howland, Sgt., 1.
Howitt, Capt. (Bde.-Maj.) H. G., D.S.O., M.C., 148, 169, 178.
Hunt, Lieut. C. B., 25, 29, 64, 65.

Infantry Hill, 105.
Isbergues, 177, 194.
Itchin Farm, 212.

Jones, Capt. H., M.C., 44, 100, 101, 117, 162, 171, 172, 211.
July 19th, 1916, Operations of, 12, 13.
Junction Post, 214-216.

Kemp, Lieut. S. F., M.C., 175, 186.

INDEX

Kilby, Sergt., 100, 101.
Kirk, Lieut. J., 175, 193, 198, 203.
Kettle, Sgt., 190.

La Gorgue, 10, 212, 214.
La Lacque, 194.
La Motte, 169-171.
La Pierre au Beurre, 185, 188.
La Pierrière, 189, 197-199.
Languevoisin, 164, 165.
Laventie, 8, 10, 176, 214-216.
Lawson, Lt.-Col. A. B., D.S.O., 163, 169, 188, 191.
Leatherbarrow, Sergt. J., 98, 101, 117.
Les Amusoires, 179, 181, 182, 196.
Les Fosses Farm, 107.
Le Vergier, 84, 85.
Liettres, 199.
Lindsey, Lieut., 109.
Linghem, 198, 216.
Lodge, 2/Lt. T., M.C., 175, 181, 186, 187, 189.
Loewe, Lieut. L. L., 43.
Longford, Pte., 26, 66.
Longley, Pte., 66.
Lyon, Lieut., 44.
Lys River, 176, 212, 213.

Mackenzie, Maj.-Gen. Sir Colin, K.C.B., 49, 165, 195.
Maison Ponthieu, 42, 45, 49.
Maissemy, 81, 90, 163.
Marcelçave, 49, 169, 170.
Marchélepot, 56, 60, 79.
Marcon, Capt. C. S. W., 57.
Maresches, 219.
Martinsart Wood, 31, 33, 34.
Matthews, Capt. C. S., 117, 159.
Merville, 8, 10, 17, 176, 177, 179, 182, 188, 201, 204, 212.
Miller, Capt. J. G. R., 186.
Moated Grange, 17.
Moberly, Capt. W. H., D.S.O., 9, 117, 125, 150, 151, 165, 166, 172.
Monchy-le-Preux, 105, 106.
Montolu Wood, 81, 86.
Monument, at Fayet, 90, 171.
Moorat, 23.
Moore, Capt. (Bde.-Maj.), L. G., D.S.O., 92, 93, 98.
Moore, Col.-Sgt., 1.
Mouquet Farm, 23, 35, 36.
Moss, C.S.M., 188.
Mowby, Sergt. W., 100.
Mudd, C.S.M. A. J., 211.

Muir, Lt.-Col. J. B., D.S.O., 158.
Murray, Capt. (Q.M.) W. G., 159, 172, 175, 193, 197.

Nesle, 168, 169, 175.
Neuf Berquin, 201, 204, 211-213.
Neuve Chapelle, 10.
Neuvillette, 20, 104.
Nicholas, Bde.-Maj., 220.
Nieppe Forest, 177, 178, 201-206, 209.
Noc River, 20, 179, 181, 198.
Noeux, 111, 112.
Northampton, 3.

O'Connor, Lance-Cpl., 100.
O'Meara, Lieut. R. A., M.C., 155, 185.
Omignon River, 79, 84.
Offoy, 165, 166.
Orderly Room, 210, 211.
Oxford, Battalion billeted in colleges, 2.
Oxfords, 6th, 159, 187.

Pagan, Brig.-Gen. A. W., D.S.O., 176, 183, 196, 198.
Palmer, Sgt., 117, 137.
Parkhouse Camp, 6.
Parsons, Sgt., 43.
Patrols, 29, 40.
Plate Becque, 201, 204, 210.
Pond Farm, 122, 124, 125.
Ponne Copse, 86.
Poperinghe, 115, 119.
Portuguese, 177, 178, 187, 194.
P.U.O., 197.
Pym, Bde.-Maj., 33.

Raid, at Ablaincourt (by enemy), 58, 63, 64.
 ,, by A Coy., 15.
 ,, by B Coy., 9.
 ,, by C Coy., 191.
 ,, by D Coy., 92.
Rainecourt, 49, 77.
Ravenscroft, Sgt., D.C.M., 201.
Regina Dug-out, 26.
Regina Trench, 25, 27, 30, 38.
Riez Bailleul, 17, 19.
Robecq, 19, 20, 177-184, 187, 188, 196.
Roberts, Pte., 66.
Robinson, Capt. A. J., 14, 23, 25, 38, 51, 56, 160, 171, 189, 191.
Rockall, Corpl., 29, 61.
Rose, Maj. D. M., 14.

INDEX

Rowbotham, Capt. G. V., M.C., 159, 160.
Rowbotham, Lance-Cpl., 66, 137, 139, 140.
Rowlerson, Lieut. G. A., M.C., 191, 215.
Ruthven, Maj. W. L., 43.

Sailly-sur-la-Lys., 212, 216.
St. Hilaire, 199, 200.
St. Hubert, 218.
St. Omer, 195.
St. Pol., 174, 177.
St. Quentin, 82, 87, 89, 90, 103.
St. Venant, 176, 178, 181, 183, 187, 196.
Schuler Farm, 122.
Scott, Lieut. W. D., 7, 117, 119, 124.
Selency, 90, 160, 162.
Sepmeries, 218.
Shields, Capt. (M.O.), 197.
Shilson, Capt. J. W., 211.
Short, Pte., 66.
Sloper, Sgt., M.M., 101, 117.
Smith, Pte., 66.
Smith, C.S.M. S., D.C.M., 211.
Soyécourt, 81, 82.
Spresiano Camp, 204.
Stanley, Capt. J., M.C., 185, 188, 215.
Stobie, Capt. W., O.B.E., 26, 79, 106, 169.
Stockton, Capt. J. G., 7, 23, 43, 51, 84, 117, 124.
Suffolks, 5th, 209, 211.
Sunken Road (Fayet), 90, 94, 96, 161.
Suzanne, 155, 156.
Symonds, Capt. R. F., 203, 210, 219.

Taylor, Lieut., 97, 100, 101.
Taylor, C.Q.-M.S., 193.
Tertry, 81.
Thomas, 'Benny,' 144, 159.
Thompson, Pte., 66.
Thorne, Brig.-Gen. A. F. A. N., C.M.G., D.S.O., 219.
Tiddy, Lieut. R. J. E., 7, 15.
Tilly, Lieut., 86.
Timms, Pte., 25, 63, 66.
Transport, the, 192-194.

Tremellen, Lance-Cpl., 75.
Tripp's Farm, 196.
Tubbs, Capt. A., 94.
Tullock's Corner, 36.

Ugny, 159, 164, 165.
Uzzell, Lance-Cpl., 64.

Vendegies, 218.
Verlaines, 166, 168.
Vermandovillers, 77, 79.
Viggers, Corpl., 76, 97, 140.
Villers Bretonneux, 169, 171.
Vlamertinghe, 120.
Voyennes, 165, 166.

Waldon, Col.-Sgt., 1.
Wallington, Lieut. C. H., M.C., 151, 160.
Warwicks, 2/6th, 179.
  „   2/7th, 181.
Watkins, Sgt., 82, 84.
Wayte, Lieut. J. P., M.C., 85, 86.
Webb, Lieut. E. S. F., 117.
Weller, Lieut. B. O., 157.
Wetherall, Lieut.-Col. H. de R., D.S.O., M.C., 104, 111, 132, 150, 187, 196, 203, 204.
White, Brig.-Gen. the Hon. R., C.B., C.M.G., D.S.O., 15, 39, 48, 93, 112, 121, 145-148, 163, 165.
Wilcox, Lance-Cpl. A., V.C., 215.
Wieltje, 132, 134.
Williams, Col.-Sergt., 1.
Willink, Capt. G. O. W., M.C., 169.
Wiltshire, Lieut. G. H., 149.
Winchester Post, 10.
Winnipeg, 122.
Wise, Lance-Cpl., 140.
Wood, R.S.M. T. V., 1.
Woodford, Lieut. G. W., M.C., 193.
Woulfe-Flanagan, Lt.-Col. F. M., C.M.G., D.S.O., 203, 220.
Wright, Bugler, 66.
Writtle, 4.

Young, Capt. R. E. M., 211.
Ypres, 58, 119, 120.

Zeder, Lieut. J. H., D.C.M., 7, 9.
Zollern Redoubt, 36, 38.

The Naval & Military Press Ltd

www.ingramcontent.com/pod-product-compliance
Lightning Source LLC
Chambersburg PA
CBHW071814230426
43670CB00013B/2456